SUPPORTING STORIES
being a teaching assistant

SUPPORTING STORIES
being a teaching assistant

Celia Dillow

Trentham Books

Stoke on Trent, UK and Sterling, USA

Winner of the IPG DIVERSITY Award 2010

Trentham Books Limited
Westview House   22883 Quicksilver Drive
734 London Road   Sterling
Oakhill   VA 20166-2012
Stoke on Trent   USA
Staffordshire
England ST4 5NP

First published 2010

British Library Cataloguing-in-Publication Data
A catalogue record for this book is available from the British Library

ISBN 978 1 85856 481 4

Designed and typeset by Trentham Books Ltd and printed in Great Britain by Henry Ling Ltd, Dorchester

CONTENTS

Foreword

Human beings are storying beings. We live by stories, making sense of our perceptions and experiences by creating narratives which we can then share with others.

In this book Celia Dillow tells stories by and about teaching assistants, stories about what they do, why they do it and the meanings the work has in their lives. This is an important book.

Despite all the rhetoric, planning and policy that has surrounded the development of a job that has come to assume increasing significance in British classrooms, there would still seem to be a widely held view that teaching assistants simply 'help out' in classrooms. These stories show that this is far from the case. They also challenge the idea that classroom assistants would be teachers if they could.

I enjoyed reading the book and I learned a lot from it. I'm sure others will too.

Pat Sikes
Professor of Qualitative Inquiry,
University of Sheffield.

Introduction

Narrative is the way we remember the past, turn life into language and disclose
to ourselves and others the truth of our experiences. (Ellis, 2004:126)

Storytelling is a uniquely human activity and resource. We are charmed
by stories and entertained by them. They are the way that we share our
lives and experiences and make culture visible.

Educational research is peppered with the language of the storyteller. Often it
promises to tell us tales, sometimes it promises action, drama and mystery. It
always intends to inform us. This book focuses on the stories that were told
during one small piece of educational research. It tells of an ethnographic
study of teaching assistants (TAs) in primary schools; and then it tells their
stories.

The study itself examined the lived experience of a small group of primary
school TAs. It sought to go beyond quantitative data in order to provide
insight into who they were and how it felt to do their job. It stitched together
stories, feelings and history; pain, frustration and fun; everyday lives and
everyday politics. It exploited the magic of the storyteller in order to evoke
real characters, settings and lives. It presented the research findings as a series
of short stories, each one about a TA working in a primary school.

The book is divided into three sections. Part 1 describes the research project.
Chapter 1 is devoted to the TA and puts her* into historical, cultural and political context. It examines how the work has changed and includes descriptions
of the various roles, based on local authority resource documents and model
job profiles. Chapter 2 contains information about the research project and
how it was carried out. There are notes on the characters and settings as well
as brief descriptions of research methods and approaches.

The stories themselves form the heart of the book and can be found in Part 2,
Chapters 3-15. There is one story in each chapter.

Part 3 offers discussion and reflection on the process and on the product. It grounds the stories in the data and presents some ways to start thinking about them. It makes explicit some guidance for good practice and offers advice about managing the partnerships between classroom practitioners. Chapter 16 is divided into two sections: Advice for TAs; and Advice for schools. Each section is summarised in a series of key points and questions.

The book closes with a sequel which emphasises that this is a study about real people and lives. I follow up our main characters to find out who is doing what, and where, two (and more) years after our initial contact.

Notes
The book makes use of some storytelling devices, for example flashback, real speech and narrative passages within the main text. These can be identified by bold or indented text.

Names and place names have been changed and random pseudonyms have been assigned in order to protect individual identities.

*She or her is chosen consciously throughout the text. This does not represent gender bias but merely reflects the fact that nearly 98 per cent of TAs are women and that the participants in this small study were all women.

Acknowledgement
This research project was completed at the University of Sheffield and was enabled by a studentship from the Economic and Social Research Council.

PART 1
THE RESEARCH PROJECT

Confidence can be induced by a description of methods
(Polkinghorne, 2007:481)

1
TA matters. TAs matter

'What did you say you were studying, Celia?' Annie was being friendly and we were just making conversation at the school gate, but my heart slumped at the prospect of having to explain it – there were no neat explanations. 'Well – basically – teaching assistants – and what it feels like to be one', I say, as neatly as possible. 'Why are you doing that then?' she asked, already scanning the tousle headed children squeezing out of the school doors. 'They are quite important', I falter and then, 'they are being used in schools these days in lots of ways – I bet Ben and Ollie have sessions with Mrs Lewis don't they?' Annie nods distractedly, I can see the 'so what' question forming behind her polite interest so I finish with a rush, 'and not everyone welcomes that; teachers sometimes resent them; parents don't know about them; the government keeps on mentioning them. Sometimes it seems like everyone is talking about them and expecting all kinds of things of them. So I am interested in who they are and what it feels like to be them'. The moment is lost as we are swept along in the end-of-school drama.

'What have you done today? She said what? Did you do that all by yourself? Who wants to come to tea? Yes, Cubs tonight, piano tomorrow – no, no swimming. Where's your kit/lunchbox/coat ...?'

What else did I want to say to Annie? I have been an assistant in a classroom and I found it tough, delightful, funny and boring. I had to learn new skills, think on my feet and make it up as I went along. I was exhausted and energised; welcomed and valued and underpaid. I was in the way and needed by everyone. I watched the clock but did not have enough hours in the day. I was bored and depressed by the repetitive, menial nature of emptying the dishwasher and sharpening pencils; yet challenged by teaching, explaining, questioning, performing, observing, planning and assessing. The whole role is beset with contradictions, and contradictions make for interesting investigation.

The subject of TAs is political and Political. For many years TAs were unseen and unregarded. Watkinson has referred to their historical invisibility and to the lack of status the role has endured until recently (Watkinson, 2003), indeed, it was only in 2000 that the term Teaching Assistant was adopted to describe, 'those in paid employment in support of teachers in primary, special and secondary schools (DfEE, 2000:4). Until then they had many names, but no single agreed-upon and recognised label.

However, since the school workforce reform (DfES, 2003) their profile has been raised and so has their presence in classrooms throughout the land. They are concrete evidence of the ways staffing in schools is changing, their role is associated with the vital matter of raising standards in our schools. They have been a crucial part of the government's reform and modernisation agenda although their increased role and number has been construed as a threat to professional identity and status by some teachers and teachers' unions.

To put TAs into classrooms is not a new idea, it reflects common sense, pro-verbial wisdom that 'many hands make light work' as well as pedagogical wisdom that a higher adult:child ratio in a classroom is helpful. In the 1960s the Plowden Report (CACE, 1967) reflected this concern about class size in its recommendations for the recruitment and training of many more teachers' aides. Plowden had children at its heart but it also commented on shortages of teachers.

The balance between serving the needs of the child and serving the needs of the teacher is still a key part of debate about TAs today, as are the inherent tensions. Plowden, for example, noted that teachers desired to have ancilliary help but did not want untrained staff 'diluting' the profession. In the 21st Century, some teachers and teaching unions are still resistant to the idea that there might be crossover between the work of teachers and TAs, for example most (89%) objected to the suggestion that assistants could cover for teacher absence according to an Institute of Education survey (Neill, 2002). Demarca-tion between teachers and TAs is debated now as it was then, 'there are almost insoluble difficulties in defining what is and what is not teaching and what can and cannot be done by ancillary staff' (CACE, 1967, chapter 24 no pagina-tion). Watkinson says that it is clear that TAs do something that could be called teaching and that this has long been a contentious issue (Watkinson, 2003).

The contention is not easy to resolve. The arguments have not gone away, but neither has the pressure to increase numbers of TAs. Government Green Papers in 1998 and 2001 emphasised support staff recruitment, training and development. Strides have been made towards an over arching scheme of qualification; pay and status is firmly on the workforce reform agenda. TA numbers have grown exponentially in the last decade and they have been the focus of several long term and detailed research reports and consultations (see for example Lee and Mawson, 1998; Hancock *et al*, 2001; Smith *et al*, 2004; Blatchford *et al*, 2004, 2006 and 2007). These reports tell us much about how they are working and what they are doing. They give us quantitative data about TAs but they do not give us the experiences and stories of the TAs themselves. Watkinson says, 'in early reports, the TA had been described rather as another piece of equipment in the school. The TA as a person with desires, experiences, capacities or competencies which could be tapped or developed was largely ignored' (Watkinson, 2003:24).

This text concentrates on the TA as a person because her life, history, desires and experiences impact upon the TA that she becomes. And TAs affect the business of the classroom. It is also true that much of the tension that underpins discussion of their deployment and employment seems to stem from a wrong identification of who they are and what they want. They are not would-be teachers or teachers on the cheap. Some regard the role as a route into teaching, indeed some teacher training institutes recommend experience as a TA to potential applicants, but many are happy to be assistants. If antipathy towards assistants from teachers and teaching unions stems from anxiety about a breach of the professional borders, then some information about them may help to allay fears. Familiar faces are not usually as threatening as strangers.

In order to open up the area of the border skirmish even further, a certain amount of deconstruction is required. TAs are usually seen in a binary relationship with teachers. The dominant discourse, particularly during the process of workforce reform, is that they are being made available to address the problems in teacher work and life balance, recruitment and retention. For example in discussion of the use of TAs to cover teacher absence, England schools Minister Jim Knight said, 'teaching assistants *eased the burden on teachers*, but should not lead classes for more than a short period' (BBC, 2008, my emphasis). They ease this burden by taking on routine clerical and administrative tasks and by providing cover for absences and non-contact time. This has led to debate about which tasks define teaching and teachers and so a list of 'specified work' was drawn up as part of the national workload agreement (DfES, 2003). It lists tasks relating to teaching and learning which may be carried out by support staff providing that they are done under the direction and supervision of a teacher. It includes activities that look like teaching, for example planning, preparing and delivering lessons and assessing work.

However, interpretation of this advice is blurry and depends on individual schools and managers. Therefore, TAs are regularly carrying out many tasks that demand high level teacherly skills, while also undertaking the routine administration and housekeeping such as the cliched washing paintpots. The mixed nature and level of skills required for these jobs is complex, some are professional and some are routine. For this reason it is interesting to investigate the people who are doing them. How do they think and feel about their work and lives? What is it like keeping their roles in tension? How are they coping? This book seeks to switch the focus from teacher to TA and to show who the assistant is and what it feels like to be one. This study concentrates on the TA's experience and puts her centre stage by telling her stories. The stories (in Part 2) enlarge the discourse of workforce reform by including the experiences of those who are involved at its heart, in the classroom.

Changing roles

Two striking features of the employment and deployment of TAs are the extent to which the role has developed recently, and the speed with which this change has taken place. In the 1998 and 2001 Education Green Papers, the government committed itself to an increase in the number of TAs that would be working in schools (DfES, 1998; DfES, 2001). In January 2003 the government, local authority employers and the relevant trades unions (with the exception of the National Union of Teachers) signed the National Agreement, *Raising Standards and Tackling Workloads* (DfES, 2003) which contained features designed to address the problems faced by overburdened teachers. The recruitment and deployment of many extra support staff was one of these features.

In October 2002 the Secretary of State for Education and Skills heralded a revolution in the nature and extent of work done by assistants in schools. A Consultation Document called *Developing the Role of School Support Staff* was launched to seek responses to questions about the use of support staff in schools. It proposed, 'for the first time to regulate the involvement of support staff in teaching and learning' (DfES, 2002:5) and promised, 'a system confident enough to sweep away old demarcations and assumptions' (*ibid*:9). The notion of sweeping away old demarcations characterises the optimism of the document. It looks forward to an era when highly trained, professional teachers would oversee well organised teams of support staff to, 'drive forward new, more flexible models of teaching and learning' (*ibid*:9).

The final report, published in April 2003, says that there was a positive response to the consultation and that most respondents, 'found the vision compelling' (DfES, 2003b). Since then the pace of change has barely slackened. According to the Annual School Census (ASC), the full time equivalent number of TAs in the primary phase in 2005 was 95,460, a figure which is double that recorded in 2000 (ASC, 2006), provisional figures for 2008 have risen to 115,000 (DCSF, 2008). Funds for training were ring fenced within the new School Development Grant. The investment was not only financial it seemed to be pivotal to workforce reform. The General Teaching Council (GTC) acknowledged that, 'the policy shift towards involving a range of other adults in teaching and learning is well underway' (GTC, 2003:3).

Teaching is changing too. It has changed since the Conservative Government's Education Reform Act in 1988. Market forces were brought to bear on school management, together with a National Curriculum, standardised assessment and schools' performance league tables. Subsequent education policy under New Labour governments has continued to emphasise choice, diversity, centralised regulation and prescription (DfES, 1998). Policy changes have affected what teachers actually do. Nixon says, 'the language of inputs and outputs, of clients and products, of delivery and measurement, of providers and users, is not just a different way of talking about the same thing. It radically alters what we are talking about. It constitutes a new way of thinking about teaching and learning. Ultimately, it affects how we teach and how we learn' (Nixon, 2005:245).

One facet of the new management of education was a steady increase in the burden of paperwork. Record keeping and form filling threatened to keep teachers away from doing the parts of their jobs that they more readily regarded as professional teaching. There was discussion about morale in the teaching profession and concerns about teacher recruitment and retention. The *Teacher Workload Study* (PWC, 2001) suggested that teachers would benefit from reduced workloads and that support staff could be used to reduce them .

The remodelling process generated a list of tasks that teachers should no longer be required to do. These included collecting money, checking absences, bulk photocopying, copy typing and producing standard letters, keeping records, filing, classroom display, analysing and processing exam results, collating student reports, administration associated with work experience and teacher cover, ICT trouble shooting, commissioning new ICT equipment, ordering supplies and equipment, stocktaking, cataloguing, preparing, issuing and maintaining equipment and materials, minuting meetings, co-coordinating and submitting bids, seeking and giving personnel advice, managing and inputting pupil data (DfES, 2003). More support staff could definitely help to ease the burden.

It is interesting that the need for TAs is the result of government policy as well as a crucial plank of it. Teachers could not teach and comply with the additional burden of administrative tasks brought about by a change in managerial direction. Therefore more TAs were commissioned as an integral part of that managerial change. It is here that I see some confusing thinking about TAs and what they are for. They are put in classrooms to reduce the pressure of intensification, and then because they are there, they are used to take on teacher-like roles, and in many cases they have done them well. As Whitty says, 'while the remodelling agenda has seen administrative roles reallocated from teachers to support staff it has also seen a 'reaffirmation' of the new role of teaching assistants' (Whitty, 2006:7). This leads to questions about where the boundaries are between teacher and assistant. Despite the National Agreement's assurance that teachers and support staff are not interchangeable (DfES, 2003) the boundaries are difficult to discern, or are, 'rather porous' (TAWG, 2001).

This blurring of boundaries is not good for teaching assistants. Presently they are employed as assistants and yet one in three say that they are not being supervised by anyone; two thirds regularly work more hours than their contract says and there is still little evidence that they are receiving more training (Blatchford *et al*, 2007). They may be required to teach although they are not paid to do so. TAs are now being used in jobs that look like teaching, as well as in more traditional 'assisting' tasks. Therein lies the paradox. They have been called into being in order to reduce the burden on teachers, but by pushing the boundaries of what a TA may do, the notion of what a teacher is for has been stirred up and remade too. One teacher said, 'the jobs that the TAs used to do nobody does now so that's left with you, whereas before you had somebody to mix your paint, do all those other tasks, now you don't and you have to do it yourself' (Kessler *et al*, 2005a:13). Routine tasks are now being reallocated (back) to the professional.

We have been left with two cadres of classroom practitioner and an uneven and *ad hoc* sharing of tasks between them. Territorial claims, fuelled by misunderstandings, are inevitable. For example the National Union of Teachers (NUT) refused to support the workload agreement because it represented a threat to the professionalism of teaching. Of all the proposals for expanding the use of TAs, 'the most unpopular was the proposal that assistants should cover for teacher absence (89% against)' states an Institute of Education analysis on behalf of the NUT (Neill, 2002:4). The topic is current and views are polemic. A decision perhaps needs to be made about whether we have a pedagogical need for 'teaching assistants' or a managerial need for 'teachers' assistants'.

A note on HLTAs

This distinction may in future be catered for in the Higher Level Teaching Assistant (HLTA) training and accreditation programme. Some 21,000 TAs have now gained the higher level status (TDA, 2008). HLTAs can expect to hold positions of greater complexity and autonomy and work alongside teachers on teaching and learning tasks. In order to achieve accreditation they need to provide evidence that they meet 31 professional standards relating to values and practice; knowledge and understanding; and teaching and learning activities (TDA, 2007). Deployment is at the discretion of the headteacher, but could mean that HLTAs do some teaching under the direction of a teacher. This has local and historical implications. In some schools TAs have to contend with inherited understandings about what they are for, and some individual TAs with aspirations to take on more responsibility may have to move schools in order to find HLTA level work.

I suspect that this dual track approach to TAs and their training and recruitment could go some considerable way towards solving the ambivalent nature of TA work, with TAs taking on the general assistance roles and HLTAs doing the higher level, teacher-like roles. But at the moment deployment is patchy with a third of HLTAs being used (and paid) for only some of their hours as HLTAs (Wilson *et al*, 2007). In practice, because of the nature of staffing in schools, assistants carry out split roles, in other words a mixture of HLTA and non-HLTA duties. A lack of specific HLTA roles in schools, together with lack of understanding of the status, were considered to be major barriers to the effective deployment of HLTAs by the recent National Foundation for Educational Research/Training and Development Agency for Schools report (Wilson *et al*, 2007).

None of the TAs who appear in the stories in this book had achieved HLTA status, although one was working towards it. However, all were carrying out a variety of HLTA duties. Some had felt discouraged from pursuing it, and had even inferred that if they achieved the status, they could not be paid at HLTA level in their present schools. There is often no extra money in school budgets to pay a higher salary and if TAs want to be paid at the HLTA rate, the school can only afford to pay them for fewer hours

What TAs do

TAs assist. Underpinning this is the common sense view that another adult present in the classroom will improve the experiences of children and teachers, and that this will have a positive impact on standards of achievement. However research evidence is ambivalent. An Open University study into the employment and deployment of TAs found that, 'although there was a widespread personal belief that assistants were a good thing ... research evidence is supportive rather than conclusive' (Hancock *et al*, 2001:6).

Furthermore, the EPPI-Centre (Evidence for Policy and Practice Information) carried out a systematic review of international literature that focused on the impact of support staff in classrooms, and suggested that the notion of impact was complex (Howes *et al*, 2003). It could not be measured solely in terms of overall achievement. The review used evidence from large studies (for example Gerber *et al*, 2001; Blatchford *et al*, 2004 and 2006) to show that extra adult support had, 'no clear and consistent effect' (Howes *et al*, 2003:35) on class attainment scores. Mujis and Reynolds found that the assistants had only minimal effect on the mathematics achievement of low achieving pupils in primary schools (Mujis and Reynolds, 2003). The main barrier to effectiveness was considered to be lack of planning and liaison time between teacher and TA, with the qualifications, training and status of the TA also having an effect (Moyles and Suschitzky, 1997; Lee, 2002; Wilson *et al*, 2002).

However, while quantitative evidence for a positive impact is weak; qualitative evidence, which takes into account the perceptions of headteachers, teachers and children, is much more supportive. A broadening of the notion to include impact on individual children and families and impact on working environments and relationships, does bring positive evidence of improvement. Research in the Classroom Assistant Project (CAP) in Scotland builds on these broader, qualitative understandings, by examining the changing attitudes of parents, teachers and pupils. Here evidence suggests that assistants, 'can make a strong contribution by improving the quality of learning in the classroom, by having a positive impact on the personal and social development of pupils, and by encouraging parental involvement in their children's learning' (Woolfson and Truswell, 2005:74).

Two types of TA

The National Joint Council for Local Government Services (NJC) negotiated with local authorities and the relevant trades unions to draw up guidance for schools on the work of their support staff. The guidance included advice on contracts, training, development and model job profiles which could then be used by local authorities to produce job descriptions and grading schemes (NJC, 2003). These model profiles identify three 'families' of support staff roles: teaching assistants, administration/organisation and curriculum/ resource support.

The teaching assistant family is further divided into two strands, one of which covers teaching support and classroom based activity and the other covers pupil support roles and behavioural guidance and monitoring. Each 'family' of roles is then categorised by skills levels. There is an Induction Level 1 of basic skills for those working under the close direction of a Teacher or TA manager. The tasks increase in autonomy and esoteric knowledge up to a Level 4 job, which has management responsibility. The skills levels are linked to the National Qualifications Framework, for example a Level 3 job would require a National Vocational Qualification (NVQ) 3 (or equivalent), a Level 4 job would be for a Higher Level Teaching Assistant (HLTA).

Teaching Support

The highest numbers of support staff are employed in supporting teaching and learning in the classroom. (HMI, 2002; DfES, 2003). Almost invariably, roles are worked out at local level, between teacher and manager, with head-teachers having overall responsibility for deployment (Smith *et al*, 2004), but some broad themes and similarities can be drawn out of the data. A common trend is the move away from a traditional understanding of an extra pair of hands in the classroom to wash paintpots, handle paperwork and organise resources. Many assistants now find that they spend longer supporting learners and learning than they do on administrative or welfare tasks or on managing or preparing materials.

The introduction of the National Literacy and National Numeracy strategies has caused a change in the way that TAs are used (HMI, 2002) and a greater prescription of teacher activities has lead to more clearly defined roles, with assistants playing an integral part in the running of the daily structured numeracy and literacy lessons. During the whole class input the TA helps with

11

the monitoring and managing of behaviour and is available to sit alongside pupils who might need help and encouragement to participate. When the lesson is divided into small groups, which is a key feature of the teaching of the National Literacy and National Numeracy strategies, the TA is available to work with a group of pupils. She may take responsibility for the delivery of the teacher's plans (HMI, 2002). This means circulating in the group, checking that everyone gets started, can manage the task and keeps working. The TA uses the skills of a teacher, observing, questioning and explaining, in order to monitor learning. The TA marks completed work and provides help and explanations for corrections. Outside of the National Literacy and Numeracy strategy lessons the TA may be used to help with handwriting practice or with reading; she may be involved in running practical sessions such as cookery and art, overseeing the use of computers or play activities or topic work (Smith *et al*, 2004; Woolfson and Truswell, 2005).

Pupil Support

Pupil support roles that encompass behavioural guidance and monitoring use the second highest number of assistants (DfES, 2003). A very common role for the assistant in the classroom is to work alongside disruptive children, particularly those whose behaviour is challenging. By close focus, perhaps on a one-to-one basis, on the behaviour of single pupils the assistant allows the teacher to concentrate on teaching the rest of the class. The experience of the whole class is enhanced because of the removal of distracting behaviour, and the learning experience of the disruptive pupil is enhanced because individual, adult attention is lavished upon him or her.

The assistant also plays a role in upholding discipline and behaviour policies in the whole school. The TA may supervise behaviour in the playground, at lunchtime or in assembly, for example correcting unfair or unkind behaviour by encouraging turn taking, or by modelling and encouraging good manners. The assistant takes her cue about what is tolerated from the other staff, and from the ethos and atmosphere of the school. For example, as a TA I observed the teachers and other staff members closely, noting which behaviours they acted on and how they did it. I noted the language that they used to encourage children to sit quietly, wait in line or take turns. Other tasks associated with pupil support include talking and listening to children, tending to minor injuries, initiating and participating in games and running health promotion schemes (Woolfson and Truswell, 2005).

Pupil support roles differ, of course, across the age phases. Wilson notes that younger children need more help with practical tasks, whereas in classes of older children help is often focused on an individual child (Wilson *et al*, 2002). Infants, for example, need much more practical help to put-on, take-off, do-up or undo their shoes, coats and sweaters. The assistant spends time looking for missing lunch boxes, snacks, PE kit, coats, reading books, home-work and wellies. She plaits hair, ties shoelaces, takes children to the bath-room and checks nametapes to find out who is wearing the wrong sweater, trousers and/or tee shirt. When it comes to helping out, the children do not mind who helps, as long as someone does.

'Oh look!' exclaimed Annie, quickly scanning the book bags, 'a letter from Mrs Lewis'. 'Yes' says 6 year old Ollie, 'She's my teacher, we do reading and maths with her'. 'I think she is a helper', says older, wiser Ben. 'That's good, she has sent home a list of sums and number bonds for us to learn together', 'Cool' yells Ollie, who has not learnt to hate homework yet. The letter explains what the numeracy groups are working on and how the number bonds fit into the scheme they are tackling. 'And here is another letter about headlice', Annie groans, 'I can't bear it'. 'I've got a new reading book' says Ben brightly, 'I've gone up a stage, Mrs Lewis said I could manage purples'.

We head towards the gates of the school. Small groups of parents stand chat-ting while their children kick a ball in the playground, some take the oppor-tunity to grab a teacher, or a TA, and committee mums discuss the Christmas Fayre. The sun is low in the sky, the children are finally tired, it is time to go.

2

What, why, how, who, where?
Project background

This book is a scrapbook ethnography of teaching assistants in primary schools. It examines the lived experience of teaching assistants and seeks to broaden out the information that is available about them. It goes beyond quantitative data, which tallies what they are doing and how often they are doing it, and provides insights into who they are and how it feels to do their job. It draws on the narrative technique of the storyteller to share experiences and to evoke settings and spaces in a way that enables the reader to build up experiential knowledge of this pivotal role. It is a collection of bits and pieces, including autoethnographic writing and short stories written from ethnographic investigation into the lives and works of teaching assistants. There are first person narratives, voices of others, field notes, snippets of pop, cultural and social science writing, script and dialogue, observation notes, stories, self commentary and self reflection. I hope that they will evoke the experiences that we shared as assistants in primary class-rooms and that they will conjure up the places and the people for you.

My decision to examine the lived experience of TAs is rooted in personal experience. I was working as a TA and I was genuinely struggling with the dualities inherent in the job description, teacher's assistant or teaching assistant? There were blurry boundaries between classroom practitioners, and blurriness is usually worth investigating. I wondered whether TAs' roles could change and upgrade and also stay the same. I wondered who would be left to wash the pots and sharpen the pencils. I wanted to join the debate about TAs. I wanted to hear someone say what I was thinking and feeling. Most of all I wanted to know about other TAs. Who were they, and were they feeling and thinking this too?

My personal experience with TAs is chequered. My first job in a school was in the junior department of an American school in South America. It was a temporary job. It was something to do, in a land where jobs for ex-patriates were hard to come by, and so I became a Teacher's Aide in 2nd Grade. For the first time, I observed closely the work of a primary teacher and considered it as a career. I worked alongside individual children and small groups. I helped them to keep up and encouraged them to concentrate. I supervised the playground at lunchtime, listened to children read in English and helped with art and drama. When I returned to England, and to my office job, the idea of working in a primary classroom would not go away. In the early 1990s the use of classroom assistants was raised nationally and quickly dashed away, written off as a 'mums' army'. The sentiment and the name have been hard to shrug off (Ainscow, 2000).

There then followed the years when my involvement with TAs was as a consumer, or client. My own small children reached infant classes and I observed TAs at work. As a new member of the parent body, I was at first unsure which labels belonged to which members of staff. Sometimes it was not obvious who the teacher was and who the assistant. My most pressing concern was that my infants were gently and effectively launched into their formal education. Like most parents, if I had a concern or a 'thank you' or something to share I spoke to the professional adult most closely linked with my child; or whoever was readily available with time to listen.

I watched TAs help teachers to do the hands-on caring that infants need: help with shoelaces, buttons and belts; tying up hair and holding skipping ropes; patching up knees and quarrels; wiping tears and noses. I also received notes from TAs about reading books, school trips, nurses' visits and homework. As we progressed through school, I watched TAs listen to readers and coach small groups for tests. They did baking, puppet making, skating and drumming. They organised school holidays and ran after-school clubs. I was aware that they enriched the life of the school and I assumed that they were doing something that looked like teaching.

Sometimes I did something that looked like assisting. I was a parent helper in various classes. I listened to readers and helped small groups. I helped with messy play and read stories during quiet time. I walked up and down the road with hundreds of children on library visits. I watched teachers and TAs at work and I saw TAs behaving like teachers, socialised into the wiles and ways of the teaching staff. They used the same classroom language and jargon; they questioned and challenged like teachers; they used the same techniques for eliciting good behaviour and for managing groups and classes.

These skills have also been recognised and observed by Watkinson. She says, 'when TAs are observed in action, it is clear that they also teach' (Watkinson, 2003:127). She has listed a number of teaching skills which she says can be observed when watching TAs at work, these include: planning and preparation; performance; exposition, directions and explaining; questioning and extending; challenging, pacing and motivating; intervention and non-intervention; working with groups, individuals or a whole class; supporting practical work; resource management; multitasking; and assessment activities (Watkinson, 2003).

Eventually, I went back to school myself, and returned to the primary classroom as an undergraduate researcher. I mapped out the different tasks in primary schools in an attempt to analyse staff teams. I found TAs ordering materials, book keeping, designing play spaces, painting classrooms and managing resources. They ran libraries, organised the cupboards, accompanied residential trips and administered lunch money. They liaised with parents and governors. Sometimes they were governors, usually they were parents. They were vital members of staff teams.

When I started this project I thought that I should become knowledgeable about TAs. I should be an expert. I turned, at first, to the government and trawled its websites for information about TAs. I tracked down Green Papers and White Papers and Consultation Documents. I ordered and downloaded and traced big, thick research reports about impact and efficacy. Each document, obviously, led to new, untapped sources. I made them into fat files and settled down to read. It was a dispiriting time.

From the facts and figures presented I soon knew the average age, race, social and family status of these people, of whom 98.9 per cent are women (Hancock *et al*, 2001; Blatchford *et al*, 2006). I already knew they were people like me, but now I really knew it – I could prove it! I found out about job descriptions, training policies, mentoring and line managers. I could write lists of tasks that TAs might be expected to do. The most recent report from the *Deployment and Impact of Support Staff in Schools* project aims to produce, 'fine grained analysis of support staff' (Blatchford *et al*, 2007:104). It uses time logs completed by assistants. Tasks are grouped together into categories such as class preparation, help pupils with learning goals, support learning strategies, managing pupil behaviour. Their macro analysis of these logs tells us the length of time and the frequency with which different tasks were covered, it shows us a range of generic activities but it does not tell us actually what the TA was doing. It cannot tell us how the assistant felt as she did it; or why she was doing it; or how that activity fitted into the rest of the lesson or day. It cannot tell us whether she had prepared it or worried about it. It cannot tell us whether she understood what she was doing; or whether she did it effectively or competently or happily. It cannot tell us how the children responded, or what the teacher said. It does not tell us about moods and feelings or whether the sun was shining.

There are books of the handbook variety, aimed at TAs and TA trainers for the purpose of training and induction (eg Birkett, 2001; Burnham, 2003; Hryniewicz, 2007). They cover the behavioural, pedagogical and developmental information that TAs would need for their work. There are books for teachers and managers concerning the employment and deployment of TAs (Watkinson, 2003). These are essential. But in all of these the TA voice remains small, it stays in the background. Sometimes TAs and headteachers and teachers are quoted, occasionally vignettes or small case studies are presented and it is these voices that leap from the page and give some colour and life to the work. Here the lively accounts of the experiences of these TAs enrich the understandings about how to optimise the TAs' contribution to the pupils.

But other questions need to be addressed too. What does it feel like to be haggled over in the press? Do they mind about issues of status and pay? What is it like to go to school each day and not know what you are supposed to be doing?

Ethnography

Ethnography is an holistic method of studying peoples, societies or cultures. It values people and the stories of their lives. It uses first hand observation, participation, interviews, conversations and questionnaires in order to collect data, and it values writing as the best way to describe these findings. For this study I have drawn inspiration from traditional ethnographies. Time in the field was valued as a medium for getting alongside a community or group to catch the way they are and begin to understand the meanings that they live by and with. By spending time shadowing and observing and participating with the TAs, I captured their experience for myself as well as listening to the stories that they told me.

We met in small groups. I used a tiny digital recorder to record our conversations after establishing that the only reservations the TAs had about this was that they did not like the sound of their own recorded voices. It was an unobtrusive device, and meant that I could converse without needing to take shorthand notes at the same time. I was able to be a more natural participant in the conversation, without the reminder of my researcher status (the field-worker's notepad) constantly before us.

The conversations were arranged for times that were as convenient as possible for the TAs. This invariably meant during lunch time. I was careful to ensure that I did not encroach too heavily onto this important break in their day. We sat informally in a quiet space, drank coffee together and ate our sandwiches. We met approximately twice a month for our conversations, they took place over the course of an academic year. I settled on a minimum of two-week intervals between sessions to allow time for transcription. This also gave time and space for the process of reflection and the beginning of analysis, which was essential before preparing for subsequent sessions. I transcribed the data myself.

Hearing the voices again at home enabled me to reflect upon nuance and texture in conversions that I may have missed on first hearing. Kearney says, 'you can hear the patterns' (Kearney, 2005:154), and so I spent time listening to the voices and reading over the transcripts, listening for patterns and making links. I devised a schedule of questions to use, starting with autobiographical details and broadening out into inquiry about feelings and opinions. However I posed these questions merely as a starting point. It was not always possible, necessary or desirable to keep to them because I wanted to allow the conversations to unfold in natural ways. Without sticking to formal schedules I was able to accommodate other issues which the groups found important and these developed in organic ways, as one thought or comment led to another. During my readings about TAs, I also made notes of interesting quotations, viewpoints and areas of conflict and I was able to draw upon these to feed into our conversations. It connected us with culture and society.

One thing that surprised me during this phase of the enquiry was that the TAs were interested in each other, and often quizzed me about what, 'the others' had said: did I find that they were saying the same things as the others had? In turn I often raised questions that had arisen in another conversation. This crossover between the groups was fertile and helpful, it kept our conversations relevant and it kept them embedded in the TA culture.

My role in the sessions depended on the dynamics of the group but generally I acted as a facilitator in the discussions; asking a new question when the conversation had spent itself and refocusing when we moved completely off-topic. I also paid attention to pauses and spaces in order to invite the story-teller to continue, or elaborate, if this was appropriate. For example, in real time conversations it is important to give narrators time to rephrase something or gather their thoughts in order to express themselves more clearly. At one school, Battlefield, the conversations were one to one, but I managed them in the same way by listening, responding and keeping things going.

With all three groups I was able to be an active participant in the discussion, drawing on my own personal experience just as the others did. We started with my questions but their concerns and interests helped to shape our discussions too. In the way that women often do, we shared our lives, information about our families, concerns for the future and present day frustrations. Sometimes the conversations were so natural that it did not feel like research. When the others used me as a point of reference for what was going on elsewhere I did not feel like an expert. If I could give them a sensible answer I always felt relieved that I had not let them down. I was aware that they regarded me as someone with some kind of expert knowledge; maybe even someone who could answer their practical questions about their work and training.

In my mind I was one of them but none of us forgot that we were only there because I had instigated the sessions. This discomfort about identity in the field is not uncommon. In her search for 'autoethnographic credibility', Elaine Bass Jenks confesses that putting on the role of autoethnographer felt uncomfortable for her because she was unsure of the ethnographer's art of taking field notes (Bass Jenks, 2002). I was similarly unsure about playing the role of researcher and felt that I was always holding the roles in tension, 'I very much wanted to give the impression that I knew what I was doing' (personal research journal, 2 September 2006). I had to be both things during the conversations, a TA and a TA researcher. My occasional discomfort, reflection and realignment was a way of carving out my field identity and learning how to be and how to present myself as a researcher (Coffey, 1999).

The decision to carry out some observations came out of our conversations, they invited me in. The TAs talked eloquently about their practice and I knew that it was vital to spend time in the classroom with them, seeing for myself how their days were structured. I knew that, 'detailed observations in naturally occurring social settings' would help to capture, 'everyday realities, routines, and practical activities' (Atkinson, 2006:25) and it was this everyday-ness that I was drawn to. But I also confess that I was keen to do some observations because it felt as if it was expected of me, it was behaviour that made me look like a researcher. When I broached the subject the TAs were all very happy to be observed; they seemed to expect it and readily drew up a schedule of convenient times for me. I arranged to spend at least half a day in school with each of them, shadowing. I sat quietly in a corner and observed. I wrote in a spiral bound, shorthand notebook. I wrote shorthand notes. Like Bass Jenks (2000), I was surprised that this act, the researcher's art, drew comment from others in the school community. Teachers who had welcomed me into their classrooms because I was attached to their TAs often questioned me, light-heartedly. 'What are you writing down about us?', 'Why are you writing in shorthand, is it so we can't read what you have written?' The children, who came to my knee to observe me, were fascinated by the strange outlines and whether I could read them. But mostly I was ignored and left to scribble in peace.

From these sessions I was able to pick up the cadence and style of their interactions, and the rhythm of their working days. I watched and noted what they did and how they did it. As a researcher I looked at the surroundings and the settings and what everyone else was doing too; as a TA I observed the way they went about the business of being a TA. The teachers had agreed in advance to my presence. I wondered whether, knowing that I would be there, might affect how they planned for the day. They made nonchalant comments such as, 'Oh you are going to see a dreadful lesson today with no differentiation' and 'I forgot you were here, you will just have to take us as you find us' went some way towards reassuring me that I was getting business as usual. Perhaps my presence made them anxious: if the teachers made any comment at all, it was to voice concern that I might be forming an opinion about them and their craft, rather than that I might be interested in the work of their TAs. Mostly I was ignored.

It was fascinating to watch other people doing my job, wrestling with the same kinds of problems; how to explain this, to gain that child's attention, to accomplish these tasks. During these sessions I wrote notes to myself about how I was reacting and feeling alongside my log of observations. These form a commentary which is intertwined with the record of external events, they help to continue the business of connecting the internal and the external, they help, 'maintain a sense of moving in and out of the experience' (Clandinin and Connelly, 2000:87).

My field texts therefore comprise three different types of writing. There are the transcriptions of our recorded conversations, which I played back and typed out just like the audio typist that I had once upon a time learned to be.

There are the transcriptions of my observations that I had typed from short-hand notes; and within these are my personal reflections. My training and experience as a secretary was well used during those days.

Autoethnography

I also had my own story to tell and for this I used autoethnography, 'an auto-biographical genre of writing and research that displays multiple layers of consciousness, connecting the personal to the cultural' (Ellis and Bochner, 2003:209). Autoethnographers make use of their own lives and experiences as data. They gaze back and forth through wide-angled, outward looking lenses, and then inward, deeply inside. Relationships and institutions are examined and revealed through dialogue and action. Choice of language is very important and culture, history and positionality are included and celebrated because they affect the way that we make sense of our experiences. Autoethnography also shows how our 'personal accounts count' (Holman Jones, 2005: 764), it shows how lives are lived and experienced, it puts people first.

I experienced being a TA as a person connected to the outside world, with awareness of social and cultural sensitivities. I was a wife and mother at the school gate. I shopped in the local store, queued up at the post office, and filled up my car at the service station. My children were learning to read, preparing for tests, forgetting their lunch, losing their kit, acting, singing and dancing in school plays. They got into trouble and fell out with friends. I made costumes and cakes and arranged sleepovers and birthday parties. I supported sports days and fairs, painted faces and joined committees. I sat opposite the teacher on parents' evenings and heard about assessment and key stages and reading levels. I rang the school when they were ill, I spoke to the TA when I was worried.

As a TA I listened to readers and took small groups to prepare for tests. I found lunchboxes and PE kit, helped them to sing and dance, patched up knees and friendships, designed costumes and sets. I listened to good news about birthdays and parties, and I shared bad news about families and fears.

This is why autoethnography is so powerful. I brought to my experience, and to my reflection upon re-living that experience, a complex mix of understandings about the role that I had absorbed during my natural life in and around primary schools. Autoethnography validates this interconnectedness. Coffey notes that this interconnectedness is inevitable, 'it is totally necessary and desirable to recognise that we are part of what we study' (Coffey, 1999:37).

Writing up

I spent many hours listening to the recordings, reading the transcriptions and mining the data that I had gathered. I drew up lists of themes that arose and compared these with themes that I had noted in the literature. I realised that this was an action that came close to a traditional style analysis; I could have coded the different themes and actions. I considered chopping up the field stories I had gathered in order to organise the material thematically; these themes could arise from the data itself, or I could impose them from my wider reading.

However, this method did not seem suitable for four reasons. First of all, I thought it would not preserve the different characters of my participants; it would make them bland and faceless and would not reflect the humanity in the stories. Honouring the messy and unruly nature of human experience had been a driving force in my methodological decision making.

Secondly, I thought that such an approach would turn out rather contrived and unnaturally smooth stories. I feared that they may become homogenous and indistinct; I remembered that a rich texture and rough edges were more lifelike and that I wanted stories that would reverberate with the experiences of TAs, teachers and parents. Thirdly, I felt that chopping up the stories would detract from the evocative nature of the writing (Ellis and Bochner, 2003:240). Finally, chopping up the stories in order to make them fit abstract theories or concepts did not coincide with my inclination to treat the participants and the data ethically (see below).

An alternative way of organising the data was to write stories based on characters. This had the added appeal of recognising that as readers, our interest in a story can be engaged and maintained by the fact that we care about a character, as readers we are accustomed to character driven action (Bruner, 1986). It also seemed to be a good way of aiming for lifelikeness, and emphasised the human-ness of our experiences. My research project was based on lived experience, so I decided to base my research text on people.

I reread the data I had and reorganised it into characters. To do this I started with the observation notes that I had for each individual, and to this I added chunks of transcription from the conversation and interview data. I thought about their background and biographical details and about their voices. For each character I pulled out key phrases that they used, or memorable lines from the transcripts so that I could write dialogue, monologue or thoughts in a natural and faithful way. I wrote a detailed description of each character's appearance. And then I started to tell their stories. This proved to be easier than I had imagined it would be. The most difficult part was choosing a start-ing point; sometimes this was a key quote and sometimes there was an obvious narrative arc, the endings seemed to present themselves.

Before starting the story writing I had some preconceived ideas based on a conviction that the stories of our lives affect the type of people (and TAs) that we become. I knew that I wanted to include 'previous-life' stories to show that TAs came from wide and varied life experiences. I suspect that this was fuelled by the fact that serendipity had presented me with an actor and an ice dancer amongst the participants! I also wanted to use background-life stories in order to show the TAs as women embedded in other lives. And I wanted to show everyday, mundane experience in warm, thick detail. As I got to know the data from our interactions intimately, some story themes did present themselves. For example, Juliana's tale seemed an obvious place to show teamwork working; Claire's voice and experience were altogether more tenta-tive and unsure; Jen, up on the landing, showed the one-to-one work that so many TAs need to get to grips with.

The stories are therefore based very closely on the details that the TAs gave me, and the action that I observed. When I have written from inside some-one's head, the words and phrases are their own and they reflect sentiments that they expressed. The words that I have put into their mouths came out of their mouths in the first place.

As I worked through the stories I also kept an artistic, creative purpose in mind. I felt influenced by a bricolage, scrapbook-type, approach and I con-sciously kept the need for texture and contrast in mind. The stories presented themselves out of the characters and their words and lives, but I was also on the lookout for an opportunity to use different voices, narrative styles and techniques in order to craft an interesting and readable product.

I approached one story differently. It was written for a different initial purpose but I decided to include it here so as to add to the texture and depth of the material. Lois is a composite character. The setting is based on Pinetrees, with Juliana as a support character, the incident is one that nearly occurred at Flatlands and which we had discussed in our sessions, the character is a mix-ture of our voices and sentiments. She is an experiment. I wanted to see how this type of writing could work and whether it could be included. The voice of Lois is probably mine. I think she earns her place among these stories metho-dologically. The use of composite characters is often advocated (eg Ellis, 2007) as a method of overcoming ethical issues such as anonymity; it is also a very flexible mode to work in because the writer is in control of the action.

However, I am not convinced that it is a method that is essential in the context of this project. Lois' story brings another texture to the piece but I wonder whether our knowing that she is a composite character detracts from her power? Like the composite figures in *The Ethnographic I* (Ellis, 2004) she is therefore used alongside the others, and I own up to her.

The writing of the autoethnography was a different, but not dissimilar process. I used my journal, email messages, school correspondence, calendars and lesson plans to recreate the feelings of being back at work and back at school. I concentrated on sensations in order to bring back memories of particular situations. I remembered a series of calendar events, the school year punctuated by trips and festivals and special occasions and I concentrated on these to give a framework to the story. I set the scene richly and focused the early part of the narrative on feelings about being interviewed and going back to work.

It was the first story that I wrote, and I used it as a working document during the interviews, conversations and writing process. I chopped it up and layered it with the literature for an earlier paper and then I stuck it all back together again and edited over and over. I edited for style, verisimilitude and evocation. I thought about what I felt and stayed faithful to the feelings that I had at the time. I wrote about not wanting to be a TA or a teacher but not knowing about the possibility of being a researcher. I wrote a story without a happy ending.

Sometimes I left it alone for months, and then re-edited it again in the light of my dawning methodological understandings. Gradually I crept towards an appreciation of the interconnectedness of autoethnography. I knitted my story together with the culture we were in. The personal is connected to the cultural and autoethnography shows this. Autoethnography is autobiography that is aware of its position in the world. It shows this awareness by reflexivity. As I wrote the stories and my own story I continued to check back to make sure that I was looking both ways, both at the feelings from within and also the view from without. Using both the ethnographic stories of others and my own autoethnography helped immensely in this checking process, it enabled me to keep feelings, politics, society and culture in view.

Participants

I thought about how to recruit participants. I thought about a broad based appeal, via local authorities or in the educational press to ask for volunteers. Other research about TAs had been done via questionnaires sent out to headteachers, teachers and TAs in randomly selected schools across all strata (inner and outer London, metropolitan areas, non-metropolitan areas) of local education authorities (eg Blatchford *et al*, 2004). Other reports had reviewed research material which made reference to TAs (eg Lee, 2002). I thought about the mailings that all headteachers get. I thought about their overstuffed 'IN' trays and the burden of paperwork in our schools. I thought I might get no volunteers, or too many.

I knew that I wanted to meet TAs and not just read about them. I thought about being personal and building relationships and I thought, too, about my limited time and how hard it was to be many miles from home for long periods. I decided that my resources would be better deployed within reach of home, not wasted on travelling. I wanted to spend more time getting to know a few people well, rather than a short period of time with many, 'you'd need only a few, maybe five or six including yourself' counsels Carolyn Ellis (Ellis and Bochner, 2003:238). I knew that I did not want to repeat the anonymous, anodyne reports and comments that I had read from faceless, nameless TAs. I wanted to connect with them and this would take time. I wanted to write in a way that would connect with readers and this would take time too.

Martha and Rachel – I immediately thought of TAs that I would like to work with. One was a friend I had known for several years who had 'fallen' into becoming a TA at the school where our children had started. She had needed a job, and there was a job at school so she applied for it. She was funny, articulate and reflective. She had read drama at University and after graduation had worked as a professional actor until her babies were born. I felt sure that she was someone who would be generous with her thoughts and feelings. I have called her Martha. I also hoped that she would be interested in my storytelling approach. It mattered to me that my participants were interested in the project. I was aware from the start that the balance of 'gain' during the research project was heavily weighted towards me. I felt that if my participants were at least interested in, or even committed to (Coffey, 1999), the progress of the project then this would go some small way to redressing that balance. I wrote to Martha explaining my request and I invited her to meet me if she was interested.

Martha's colleague came to the meeting too. I have called her Rachel. Rachel was a TA at the same infant school, slightly known to me from my days as a parent at the school. I knew her as an efficient, cheery TA who was popular with the children and the parents. During the following months I got to know her as a tough and eloquent person who cared passionately about the children in her care. She had toured the world for nine years, as a professional ice dancer before retraining to work with children. She had a brisk and breezy approach and a wicked sense of humour. We met in school during their lunch hour. We used the meeting room and they made drinks and ate their sandwiches while we talked. We caught up on a year's worth of news and then I started to outline my interests and aims. Immediately, personal connections became important. Rachel asked what I was going to do next, not with the material, but with my life! I explained my adventure in Higher Education, my decision not to become a teacher and my recent experiences as a TA.

In this first meeting I realised I wanted to establish some credentials, not as an expert, but as 'one of the girls'. In a way I was choosing and creating a fieldwork identity (Coffey, 1999), but it felt more like I was choosing what not to be. I was there as a researcher, but it was important for me to try to minimise any barriers that that status may raise (Clough and Nutbrown, 2002). I was seeking natural conversations, not questions and answers on a survey sheet and therefore building a trusting relationship was important (Ellis and Bochner, 2003).

At this stage Martha and Rachel were unsure that they had anything to offer but were willing to help. They took away an information sheet about the project and I gave them time to consider their decision before meeting again to sign consent forms.

Juliana, Claire, Ellie and Jen – The snowball effect had worked in the first school, one contact had brought another. However, for my next participants my contact was with the gatekeeper, the headteacher of my local primary school. His support was important during the initial contact, he allowed me access (literally through the gates), although later arrangements were made between the TAs themselves and me. I 'had to establish the agreement of key people' (Atkinson, 2006:26). I knew the school quite well, but not the TAs. One of my children had attended the school for two years, but I had had no dealings with the TAs presently in post although I ran a lunchtime club at the school, as I was involved with parents there. And the headteacher had expressed an interest in my research project. I sent an open letter of introduction to the TAs, which the headteacher kindly copied and distributed. I believe he also encouraged his staff to meet me and gave his full support to the project. This was helpful. However, when I first heard that he had 'encouraged' participation, I was wary that I might get respondents who had been coerced by their manager, or at least that they felt they should be there.

This did not turn out to be the case, approximately half of the TA body volunteered and no pressure was put on the others to join. The headteacher took no further part in proceedings. As a courtesy I kept him informed of our progress (timescales, nothing more). He asked for no follow up information. Three TAs responded to the initial letter and another joined us after the first session. We arranged to meet. Again, we met in their lunchtime, in the school library. I outlined the project to them and they, too, were sceptical about what they had to offer but were interested in having a conversation.

The feeling in this first meeting with these participants was very different from my early session with Martha and Rachel because we did not know each other. The bonds of trust had to be built slowly (Ellis and Bochner, 2003:238). With them I was a stranger, coming in from the outside and so it took longer to establish the relaxed and intimate conversation that I was aiming for. Again, I found it useful to share my own story. It seemed democratic to do so since I wanted to question them about themselves and their lives. Also, in line with the tenor of this project, by sharing our stories we were establishing shared meanings and making connections.

Juliana emerged as the spokeswoman for the group. She was an eloquent person who was usually first to proffer answers or fill gaps and silences in conversations. She had grown up in the Potteries – a group of towns at the heart of the British ceramics industry in the 19th Century – approximately 20 miles from our school. She was one of the most experienced TAs in the group, and had forged ahead with training, most recently embarking on the two-year foundation degree for TAs. She had left school at 16 with a plan to teach dance and to study recreation and leisure management. Since then she had held a series of jobs in offices and retail and finance companies, including a car dealership. In 1995 she took maternity leave and, eventually, her two children joined the school. In 2002 she started work at the local primary school, having completed 12 months as a volunteer parent-helper.

Claire had grown up in the area, and had herself been a student at the school. Her children now attended it. She, too, had finished her formal education at 16 and had done jobs in factories, retailing, merchandising and as a travelling sales representative before taking maternity leave. She was keen to join our discussions, but did not believe that she had much to contribute. She was extremely reluctant to recognise her skills and experience as a TA and lamented her lack of formal training. When we started to meet she had not done a proper Induction Course, even though she had been working at the school for several years. She spent half her paid hours each week as the school librarian.

Jen joined our group slightly after the others, when she heard what fun we were having. She, too, was from the Potteries and had attended local schools where she had enjoyed all the practical subjects. She had finished school at the age of 16 and had spent her working life in the fashion retail world. She had ultimately become a branch manager before leaving to take maternity leave. She had one grown up son who had attended the school as a young boy. Since joining the school as a TA she had completed the National Vocational Qualifications (NVQs) Levels 2 and 3 in early years care and education.

Ellie grew up in Southern England, where she had attended local schools. She left school after completing one year of sixth form and spent the next 19 years working in industry. She had started as a Laboratory Assistant and, after further training and qualification, became a Technical Adviser, travelling around the factories and depots of the UK. She, too, had stopped work to become a full time mum, during which time she had moved to this corner of the North West midlands. Her son was now grown up, but he had attended the school, and in the way of these things, she had started as a volunteer helper and then progressed to formal employment. The school had enabled her to strengthen her mathematics qualifications, and she now planned and ran maths booster classes for year 6 each spring before the key stage tests.

Deborah – Deborah was another personal contact. She was a person I had met in another context and we had shared experiences and ideas about TAs. I had talked, very generally, about my project with her in the early days and she had remained interested in its progress, and in becoming involved. I knew Deborah to be energetic, vivacious and vibrant. She talked knowledge-ably about children and schools. Her confidence and authority in front of a group of children made her look and sound like a teacher, in other words her voice and presence, her questioning and eliciting, her instructing and ex-plaining mirrored those of the classroom teacher in style and content.

Deborah had grown up in Kent and had moved to the local area as a mother of young children. Unlike the other participants, she had worked all of her life with young children in a variety of settings: day nurseries, children's clubs, summer camps and playgroups. She was qualified to work with children with dyslexia and those with special educational needs (SEN), she was two thirds of the way through an Open University degree, which included a diploma in SEN. She had considered routes into teaching on a number of occasions, but was more interested in enabling all children to access the curriculum through her role as a TA. She enjoyed the links that she was able to make between families, school, church and community in her tiny, rural setting.

I had seven TAs, in three schools, in two counties, plus myself in another school in a different county. This seemed like a manageable number of people to work with and lives to get to know. The project was small scale but since I had an evocative aim, the intimacy of the project was its strength. It allowed me to dwell on the little things and on the small and concrete details.

I was concerned about gender and about being balanced and avoiding sexism. There are a few male TAs, very few. Nearly 99 per cent of TAs in primary classrooms are women (Hancock *et al*, 2001; Kessler, 2005b; Blatchford *et al*, 2006). So I did not seek a male participant. The story has a female feel to it and sometimes non gender-neutral language (for example 'she' and 'her') has been used. This is not an oversight on my part or a lack of reflexivity, neither should it be construed as a gender bias. It just reflects the fact that I was working with female participants, in a field where 98.9 per cent of workers are women.

We fitted the gender profile of TAs. We were a homogenous group in other ways that reflect the quantitative data too (see Lee and Mawson, 1998; Hancock *et al*, 2001; Blatchford *et al*, 2004; TA Forum, 2008). For example, we were white women, within the age range 30-50, seven out of eight of us were mothers, four of us worked at the school our children attended or had attended. Our age, gender and status reflected TAs across the land; our ethnicity reflected the areas that we lived and worked in. As we told our stories to each other, we found we had much in common; there was tacit understanding between us. This manifest itself in the use of common language, discussion about classroom processes, an innate knowledge about the business of our days. I realised therefore that these would be stories about women of a certain age and stage of life. My selection of participants had inevitably affected the type of data that I was able to elicit; but then my selection of participants was inevitably affected by the type of people that work in the field.

We were similar but we were also different. Our life experiences had taken us all over the country and to other lands. Our educational goals and achievements ranged from five Certificates in Secondary Education (CSEs) to a masters degree and our personal circumstances and personalities were distinct. This diversity helped to bring colour and texture to the bricolage of experiences that I gradually began to piece together.

Settings

Chantry Infant School – Chantry Infants is close to the centre of one of England's largest cities. It is a proud, tough city whose dour industrial face masks a warm heart. This heart has been damaged in recent generations, and it has had to remake itself in the light of changing patterns of industry across the world. Chantry Infants sits approximately 1 mile from the city centre, in a raised position above a busy thoroughfare and bus route into town. The school was founded in the early 19th century for the families of the neighbouring parish church. Today it is a Church of England (Aided) school. It is well regarded in the local community as a small, caring and successful infant school with a strong Christian ethos, 'every effort is made to make all pupils feel valued and special and, within this extremely supportive and caring climate, pupils thrive and flourish' (Ofsted, 2006). Places are sought after.

From here I observed small children moving on to the next stage of their education as confident and positive learners, my own included. They go to a variety of local junior schools, the majority seeking places at the large church school up the hill. In the messy way of big cities, the catchment area straddles large and beautiful houses of traditional local style, pleasantly situated in broad crescents and avenues alongside low rise and high rise local authority housing and a student quarter. The children and families of the school are ethnically and culturally diverse with approximately one third of each class coming from ethnic minority groups. Most, however, speak English fluently. There is a very strong and evident feeling of community. It is a happy place and the children enjoy school very much (Ofsted, 2006).

The school is an attractive building of mellow local brick with pointy gables and enormous arched blue timber doors. There is a neat playground and a tiny, well kept garden. It accepts 90 children into 3 forms, Reception, Year 1 and Year 2. Inside there are three large and bright classrooms, a panelled assembly hall and a small, cosy library. The school is well organised and tidy although the age of the building means that the roofs leak and some of the governors can remember the days of outside toilets. The parent body is supportive and organises activities and fund raisers throughout the year, they readily mobilise for maintenance tasks such as gardening, painting and decorating. Recent projects include reclaiming yard space outside and converting it into a dedicated play space for the Reception class. The staff team is small, busy and supportive with an energetic and experienced head. One of the class teachers (not the head) is male.

The look, feel, sound and smell of this school is very familiar to me because my children were happily enrolled here for four years and I had used it in an earlier, undergraduate project. The headteacher is well known to me; she is sympathetic towards research taking place in her school and welcomes students and those on work placements. It is here that we shall later meet Martha and Rachel again.

Pinetrees Primary – Pinetrees is also a Church of England school. It is a large primary school in a friendly and growing village in the north midlands. The centre of the village has few amenities beyond those clustered around the central crossroads on the busy trunk road which dashes west towards the Welsh borders. There is a petrol station, a convenience store, a takeaway, a butcher, a post office, two hairdressers and a popular public house. Regular buses take this road and link the middle sized market towns in the area. Young, bored teens inhabit the bus shelter and the car park during the evenings. They buy chips and gum and spend time talking on their telephones. Older, bored teens use the long straight stretch of road to race the old, small cars that their parents buy them to help cope with rural isolation and limited public transport. Nearby inland waterways criss-cross the countryside, showing how locally manufactured goods used to leave the area. The village sits amid gentle, rolling farmland spliced by areas of woodland.

It is an aspirational area, peopled by the families of farmers and farm workers, and those who have moved out of the Potteries towns, approximately 20 miles to the east. Staff from the university and the teaching hospitals nearby have also been drawn to the region. It is equidistant from two enormous city centres, but too far to be tempting as a dormitory. Nevertheless, the village is sprawling outwards, with several large estates of new detached homes having been built quickly in recent years. Once people have made it out there, they tend to stick and this is reflected in the slightly sedentary and inward looking attitudes of the place. The local parish church, to which the school is closely linked, is in the neighbouring, much smaller, hamlet. Considering the number of families now living in the area and the weekly visits of the vicar to the school, the regular church congregation remains resolutely small.

Pinetrees is central to the village and community and many of the children are able to walk to school. It is a happy and popular place and pupils enjoy going to school, 'pupils usually work solidly, with or without adult supervision, in an atmosphere of happy industry' (Ofsted, 2007b). The buildings and site are extensive, reflecting its recent history as a secondary school. The buildings are large and square, in the architectural style of the 1960s institutions, with lots of regular, square windows. Inside it is well kept and well worn, the classrooms are clean and inviting. The display boards are regularly and artistically kept up to date and reflect a busy school community. Lunch is cooked on the premises and always smells good here.

The school has over 300 students divided into 11 classes: Nursery, Reception, 3 mixed Years 1 and 2 classes, 3 mixed Years 3 and 4 classes and 3 mixed Years 5 and 6 classes. There are 12 teachers on the staff, there are three male members of staff (the head and two full time teachers). The school runs a popular Breakfast Club and After School Club staffed by professional play leaders. A local and oversubscribed playgroup uses a room in the school each morning and Beavers, Rainbows and Cubs use the hall in the evenings, thus creating further links with the families of the community.

The ethnic and cultural mix of children is not as broad as that of Chantry, reflecting the population of these northern midland villages. From here, at the age of 11, the children move on to a choice of three local comprehensive schools, depending on their catchment area. One or two children each year are destined for the large independent day school in a local town. Juliana, Claire, Jen and Ellie all work at Pinetrees.

Pinetrees is familiar to me as a setting because I was involved as a parent for two years. This prior knowledge is extremely useful during research and data gathering, it helps with scene setting and also with understanding the small local knowledge that comes with familiarity. Clandinin and Connelly liken this process to becoming part of the landscape, they say that a researcher needs to spend enough time in a situation to enable them to, 'grasp the huge number of events and stories, the many twisting and turning narrative threads that pulse through every moment' (Clandinin and Connelly, 2000:77).

My familiarity with Chantry and Pinetrees allowed me to join the narrative and to be aware of the, 'cascade of ghostly memories' (Clandinin and Connelly, 2000:66) that inhabited the two schools. My acquaintance with the head-teachers was the key that enabled my access. They had shown interest in my project and one had expressed an interest in, 'anything that encourages my staff to reflect on their practice'. They enabled my initial contact with the TAs and were helpful and encouraging as far as allowing me access to all areas of the school, but at no time did they attempt to interfere or intervene in the study.

Battlefield Junior School – Although Battlefield Juniors is only about 4 miles distant from Pinetrees it has a different feel and identity. It is a tiny school in a fiercely independent hamlet. When choosing a school for their children, parents can opt for either of these two neighbours although the natural catchment area comprises the families who have lived and worked here for centuries. Parents are supportive of the school, valuing its contribution to their community and to the lives of their children (Ofsted, 2007c). The choice in favour of Battlefield is often based on family tradition, with others opting for the distinctive characteristic that such a tiny school can offer.

The cultural and ethnic profile of the school is homogenous and white. The school has deep, historical connections with the local families and generations are buried in the graveyard abutting the school. It sits prominently alongside an ancient parish church whose crinkled tower is a point of reference on the surrounding purple plain. A pivotal battle in the War of the Roses was played out within sight of the church and legend says that the monarch watched the progress from the tower and fled before the final massacre. They say that the river ran blood red through the village that day.

Compared with this history, the school occupies a new building with vast picture windows gazing out across the playground to the farms and fields beyond. It has between 40-50 children on the roll and these are divided into two bright classes. The infant class (Reception – Year 2) shares two part time teachers and a TA, the junior class (Years 3-6) is taught by the headteacher and another part time teacher, with a TA, Deborah, in support. The headteacher is male.

Battlefield was a new setting for me and so my observations are based entirely on time spent there as a researcher, rather than coloured by any inside knowledge. Unlike Chantry and Pinetrees I was not aware of the narrative history of the place, memories of people and happenings did not flood into my mind (Clandinin and Connelly, 2000) as I moved about the space. My access was via my previous acquaintance with Deborah. She facilitated introductions to the headteacher and to the other staff.

Flatlands Junior School – Flatlands is the school where I worked as a TA. It enjoys a rural setting and the approach, which creeps between spiked hedges and crosses mud-crusted tractor trails, underlines a feeling of isolation. It is in the middle of nowhere. However, this would be a false impression. It is, indeed, on the edge of an empty, blue plain which gazes towards the north western corner of England but within a few miles are the straggling edges of several large northern towns. The catchment is therefore culturally diverse, encompassing those who work the land close to the school together with others who opt to travel out of town to the rural school, attracted by its peaceful setting and a strong local reputation for good quality education. It is surrounded by a string of plain, businesslike villages from whose simple semi-detached crescents the majority of the children are drawn. Few ethnic minority groups are represented in the classrooms.

The school buildings are red brick and Victorian in character with tall mullioned windows and a pointed clock tower. Inside the ceilings are high and the classrooms bright, but the space now only awkwardly accommodates a modern school: the staff room doubles up as a computer suite and some classrooms can only be accessed by walking through others. Upstairs there is a clutter of small rooms useful only for storage purposes, a new hall (for assemblies, lunches and gym) is a useful modern addition to the back of the building. Spaces in irregular shaped corridors and hallways have been used for extra teaching and study space.

There is a happy and purposeful atmosphere, 'all pupils are special in this school and they thrive in a very good learning environment that values each pupil and their individual qualities' (Ofsted, 2005). There is a reception class, a mixed years 1 and 2 class, a mixed years 3 and 4 class and a mixed years 5 and 6 class; each has about 25 children. The staff team consists of a non-teaching head, with six classroom teachers (some of whom are part time) and three part time TAs (one of whom was me). All the staff are female. They travel considerable distances to get to work, my own journey of 25 miles was not the longest commute. Of the four settings discussed, this one feels the least embedded in its community, the community around it is not immediately evident and the staff live their lives at a distance.

Note
The names of all participants and settings have been changed, and random pseudonyms have been assigned in order to protect identities. Where Ofsted reports have been quoted, their unique identification numbers have been removed.

PART 2
THE STORIES

There is no way of seeing, hearing, or representing the world of others
that is absolutely, universally valid or correct. Ethnographies
of any sort are always subject to multiple interpretations
(Van Maanen, 1988:35)

3

Sometimes you end
up in Worksop

The wind wailed down the broad grey street and was channelled through square grey buildings into the park at the end. It was a murky midland town on a murky midweek afternoon but there was one bright corner where a curious drama played out. A motley crew were unloading a large, plain van. From within came a series of flat screens and lumpy bags and ancient, battered trunks which bulged and squeaked as they moved. A period of intense physical work followed as everyone joined in the lifting and dragging and pushing and shoving. They wheeled large, covered racks up the kerb and through tall, matt black doors. The wind tugged and worried at the shreds of something flimsy as it trailed. There were feathers in the air and something like glitter in the dust.

The passengers on the green single decker bus, snaking down the high street, watched the procession and the protagonists with interest. There was a suspicion of too much eye make up on the men; there was unruly hair, beads, scarves and long floaty clothes. They played out a well rehearsed and silent routine. They had done this hundreds of times before and no words were needed. This town was new to them and yet they showed little curiosity about their surroundings, the van brought them, they fulfilled their commitments, and then they left. Sometimes you end up in Worksop.

Perhaps for the last time Martha and Nico made their way past the shoe shops and coffee bars and charity outlets that made up every town centre they visited. They joined the early evening crowd in the supermarket but they did not merge into it. Martha's well-worn but elegant flowing robes and bright halo of long, curling hair looked nothing like the leggings and fleeces and ponytails around her, and Nico's carefully nurtured goatie beard and long golden side burns looked piratical if not demonic. They moved through the queue with easy grace but, rather prosaically, they bought groceries: bread and cheese; olives and tomatoes; fruit and nuts. They went to a park bench to eat. Some people stared at them as they ate, but they were speaking their own urgent language, in their own world. 'Perhaps for the last time', the wind seemed to breathe as they packed up their picnic, carefully reserving the uneaten food for later, and strode back to the tall, matt black doors. Something like glitter was scattered under the bench.

They disappeared inside. The contents of the lumpy bags were displayed around a series of small rooms and the battered trunks spilled out their gorgeous contents. The laconic group was transformed into a purposeful unit, each going about his or her own excruciating and precise routine. Musicians were tuning their ancient, reedy instruments and practising sequences and there was a trill from tiny handheld bells, 'perhaps for the last time'.

Martha laid out her flowery baskets and frosted coronets in careful order, scraps of frail, spangled fabric hung just within reach. Her face was bewitched with silver dust and her hair was spun with moonbeams. She stepped out of her well worn robes and into a gown fit for a queen. It was heavy with things that gave it lustre and sparkle. It swept the floor and swung as she moved, making her appear to float. She loosened her shoulders and breathed deeply feeling her heartbeat slow. She was calm and centred and in control. She stepped through the heavy curtains, 'perhaps for the last time' they murmured as she passed.

Afterwards, when the rest of the world was sleeping, the group was high with adrenalin and desperately sought ways to wind down and shut down. Achingly tired, their bodies craved sleep but their minds could not let go. They floated together into oblivion. With the daylight, the large, plain van would be repacked, everything in its place, and they would move on to the next town. 'Perhaps for the last time' hissed the wind as it swept something like glitter down the high street after them.

Martha was sure she had heard the wind and the bells and the curtains whispering to her. She wondered whether Nico had heard the same song. This exhausting life, so full of glamour and magic was hard and it was taking its toll on her. She was doing what she loved but not living the way she wanted. She was a fairy queen with a carrier bag. She snatched meals on park benches and kept sleep at bay unnaturally. She had been doing it for too many years, up and down the country, across Europe and beyond. She left behind a trail of something like glitter and gathered good memories and rich experiences. But now it was time to stop. She and Nico had become very close during these months in the fairy kingdom; she really hoped that they would want the same things when they left it. Perhaps for the last time he jumped into the seat beside her to share the remains of their picnic.

Many less-glamorous years passed.

Martha and Nico tried very hard to occupy both worlds. They maintained a home and produced fine, healthy, real babies. He kept his place in the fairy realm and came back to her at weekends. Her elegant, flowing robes became evermore well worn; gradually she scrubbed the moonbeams from her hair and the silver dust from her face. Her feet were very firmly on the ground as she struggled while Nico was away. Making the benefit money stretch was a constant challenge. She was very, very lonely and very, very poor. She learned new skills and earned bits of money to help out and sometimes Nico's tours were local and they could be a real family for a few months. Their fine babies grew into fine children and before she knew it Martha was waiting at the school gate to collect them. She thought back to her life as a fairy queen and looked at the other mummies in the playground, she wondered what they would think if they knew about her irresponsible past and thought it was best that they did not know.

The school was tiny and solidly Victorian red brick, in one of the edgy neighbourhoods that straddles genteel middle class houses and urban deprivation. It was just one mile from the city centre and celebrated the diversity of its catchment area. It was set back from, and slightly above, a busy arterial road. There was a small, rectangle of playground complete with a tiny lawned garden and leafy storybook arbour. Inside there were just three small classes and the jolly, friendly atmosphere of a well run and well loved home.

It was a happy community and Martha was delighted to find herself, finally, embraced by another surrogate family. She worked every lunchtime as a playground supervisor, marshalling the children, joining in their games and curbing their dangerous excesses. She patched bloody knees and listened to their tales. She ensured that the footballs and the skipping ropes could share the space. On blustery days the children were particularly wild, reacting to the bewitching call of the wind, but Martha no longer heard the messages it breathed.

Finally the pull of the real world and his vivid and real family was too strong for Nico and he, too, left the other realm for the last time. Martha realised that one of them must earn some more money and so she approached the head-teacher and asked whether she might be considered for something in the classroom. She mentioned her previous experience in the playground and her good degree; she did not mention that she was once queen of the fairies in towns throughout the land.

At last the headteacher let her know about a vacancy. There was an elfin child in the reception class who required help and support. He needed encourage-ment to speak in sentences and personal attention as he played catch-up on the maths and English he had missed. He came to school reluctantly. Martha met him, his enormous eyes showed fear and frustration and confusion but he was bewitched by Martha, with her long flowing clothes and her halo of curling hair. He reached up and solemnly handed her the art he had been doing. As Martha opened it something like glitter trickled from its folds and caught the sun, chasing the dust particles in a sparky spiral to the floor. Martha recognised the magic, she loosened her shoulders, breathed deeply and took the stage for the next act in her own story.

TAs have varied and vivid background stories. Find out about them – use them.

4

Tell me what happens ...

Ascript: Action takes place in the staff room of a small, busy infant school close to the centre of one of Britain's largest cities. It is lunchtime. Martha is sewing, Rachel is ironing tie-dyed tee shirts for the summer play. They are eating lunch and talking to a Celia, a researcher.

Celia: Tell me what happens – not minute by minute, but ...

Rachel (animatedly. Speaks at breakneck pace): We come in and I empty the dishwasher, that's my first job, every morning, I put the kettles on and empty the dishwasher ... and usually refill it again because there are loads of cups left in the sink. It drives me insane.

Martha (supporting and affirming. Picks up the pace): Yeah, so that's always a bad start for her in the morning.

Rachel: I hate emptying the dishwasher but nobody else does it, and then we just have labels and laminating and mounting and displays and photo-copying ...

Martha: We just get on with stuff that we have left from the night before. I go straight to the classroom and put up work that has dried, things that I have been doing with the children, or there might be a display to put on the wall or put away, or toy boxes to get out for that day. If it's structured play you might have to choose your boxes.

Rachel: ... resources to get ready. If there's a maths activity or a science activity you get that ready.

Celia: And how do you know what's coming up, have you got a plan?

Martha: They will tell you in the morning ... and if nobody grabs you, you will get on with your own stuff, which is generally tidying and preparing the classroom isn't it?

Celia: You have mentioned labelling quite a few times, I am beginning to realise it's a big task ...

Martha: It's a massive task. Rachel does all the books, everybody's books for all three classes, and labels – drawer labels, peg tags, water bottles and lids.

Rachel: And at the moment, this term we are quite busy with costumes still, so when we get in we might start trying to put costumes together, piecing them together or naming the bags that the costumes are going to go in so that the teacher can give them out.

Martha: Rachel tie-dyed 60 tee shirts and shorts for the raindrops. I also make resources for the Early Literacy Support Group every day, or I need to plan what I'm going to do that day. I'm also doing speech therapy with a child so I need to prepare that. And that's just ongoing, either you prepare if you have time or you just busk it if you don't.

Rachel: And then the bell rings ...

Celia: And what time is it?

Rachel: It's ten to nine ...!

We do manage to get up to the staff room to have a cup of tea and a lot of the staff make it up there so everything changes then, doesn't it? There might be a student to show around the school or somebody arrives.

Martha: That's really when you find out what half of your day is going to be. So there might be some photocopying to do because, 'oh we are not doing that in literacy today we are doing this ... can you do it in assembly?'

Rachel: Or there might be some children that are not having a good morning, and they have cried and you are still trying to sort them out and find out what the problem is and what's going on.

Martha: We meet the parents, who always want to talk to us because the teacher is busy doing registration, and they might shout and scream at us, cry on us, laugh with us, say thank you sometimes, tell us something important about their child which we have to feed into the teacher. We're an important link.

Rachel: And that's nine o'clock then.

And all the parents have gone and we go down to the library and do the book bags. We change all the reading books – check who has read what, take out letters from home and homework to pass on and add forms and letters for parents. And then we go off to our classes and literacy begins. Everyone is together on the carpet and you are tagging really, noticing the children that are poking each other and not listening – I think that's called behaviour management.

Martha: Yes, or listening to readers – because getting through 30 readers everyday is quite tricky.

Rachel: Or going around putting the computers on and finding the programme or sorting out the books they are going to need or sharpening pencils or cleaning the guinea pig out or keeping lists for assessment.

Martha: Then we split into groups and we work with our group – usually the lower ability group, although the teachers do move us around.

Rachel: It's very hard. I don't watch the clock but I'm just desperate for them to write the date. 'Please, 'W' – yes that's 'W' – now 'E', 'D' – yes you have missed the 'D' never mind, put the 'N'" And, you know, by the time you get to the 'N' and it has taken 10 minutes you don't care anymore, just as long as it says 'DAY' on the end. You don't care what day it is, or not even 'DAY' just 'Y' will do! 'Oh, you've forgotten how to do 'Y' – round, up and put a tail on it – oh you've put the tail the wrong way – whoops, shall we try again?'

Martha (giggling warmly): And lots of other children have written half a page and got a full story and yours have got the date, and maybe the title.

Rachel: We have half an hour on a Wednesday with our teacher – when we are supposed to look at what is happening in the next week, but it never happens, this is an infant school, it's never normal is it?

Martha: Something comes up or someone is ill or the sun is shining and it is a lovely day so we want to go into the garden. So most of the time I only really feel I know what we are doing when I walk into the classroom and you listen during Big Book time while they're all being told what they're doing and you just pick it up.

Celia: What happens next?

Rachel: Playtime – we do a playtime duty once or twice a week and you make the coffee for your teacher who is out on playground duty with you and if there are any injuries you bring them and deal with them and do all the necessary paperwork for that.

Martha: I don't actually have much of a break. I have about 5 minutes because I have my special group. I do ELS (Early Literacy Support) which is an integrated programme, during break. Often I have not had time to read it fully, but I pick bits out and use my own stuff. I am also doing speech therapy with one child and trying to encourage him to speak in sentences, and helping a child with special needs.

Rachel: After playtime we fetch the milk and supervise, and then it is the numeracy hour, whole class on the carpet and we are still mopping noses or bottoms or finishing reading because we didn't get through them all before or – there's always something – and keeping an eye on who is listening and who is crawling away under the table and who is crying because they had a fall out at playtime. Or finding money or counters or blocks for the next activity, or putting up a display that we still haven't managed to do, or rinsing and re-filling water bottles. Or hiding/crying in the stock room (laughter).

Martha: We hide a lot so that we are not given any more jobs to do. We're working, because we are still sewing costumes or something but we're hiding so that we are not given any more jobs.

Rachel: The teachers do know, they do laugh, 'are you hiding?'

Rachel and Martha: 'Yes!'

Martha: And then it is lunch and we work through lunch. We could be tidying the library or sorting out structured play boxes, finishing off book bags and displays.

Rachel: If an order has come in through the day, when I get five minutes I put the order away and re-order stuff that people have said we have run out of. What else do we do – we don't do anything really do we?

Martha: We do all the art, and we like that, and we are the Design and Technology Co-ordinators which means we have to identify all the Design and Technology that is happening in the school. We have looked at the planning that each teacher has done across the curriculum and highlighted where Design and Technology occurs – just to evidence that we do it.

Rachel: I do a lot of things on the computer, don't I? I am constantly making things, eg all the reading records books, high frequency words sets, maths sets and games. And there is the new photo display board in the entrance hall to be done each week. And some of the parents want copies of those, so now I have to print out the thumbnails and check for orders and print them. We are social workers, secretaries, nurses, ambassadors, photographers ...

Celia: And in the afternoon, what happens after lunch?

Martha: Art, projects and topic work. Or we might be doing baking or sewing or book reviews or library visits.

Rachel: Or we are running an entire structured play afternoon – we decide what they will play with each session and prepare resources. We try to link it to projects or topics for the term so that the themes fit in. We rotate activities and try for a good mix each session.

Martha: And there has to be time for putting the washing machine on and washing drapes or dressing up clothes or aprons or table cloths or toys.

Celia: Does a woman never get away from the laundry?

Rachel and Martha: What do we do? Nothing! We do nothing ... !

Celia: Stop it you two ...

> It is a job limited only by the people who do it
> and the situations they find themselves in.

5

A funny thing happened ...

From outside comes the urgent sound of a silvery handbell. Martha hears its message, she straightens her shoulders and shakes out her haze of hair. Something is going to happen today. Two strangers have joined them this week. They are smiling and encouraging but Martha has not dared to feel encouraged, too much is at stake.

For two days the smiling strangers have turned up in unlikely and unexpected places; unobtrusively they have seen everything. They have spoken to everyone; probing and testing and peering into their lives and all the shadowy places. Something is going to happen today.

Stories, the sticky web of their shared lives, have already started to weave about them all. They are united by the common experience. They understand it by telling stories about it and they share meanings by performing them and refining them. Myths grow during times like these, characters are written into history. They take their place in the story box, creating a memory bank, conferring membership upon those who share them. They say that last time, a few years ago, Caroline hid the lost property, no one knows where and probably never will. She cast a spell and the whole mountain disappeared. It made the place look untidy and it made them look inefficient, so it had to go. They do not want to appear sloppy.

The trill of the bell calls Martha to her next task and she puts down her handiwork. She has nearly completed the sixty watery costumes. They have put bright pearly stitches on storm blue cloth for the dancing infant raindrops. She finds a place in the dishwasher for her mug, picks up the pile of paintings for the display board and hurries away. She meets Rachel in the dark turn of the stair and catches her wary gaze. They have prepared carefully for this, everybody has. What they do, they do excellently and now they want to prove it because doing it well is not always enough. Funding and support always need to be earned, and justified, and earned again. From the dark stairway she crosses the tiny entrance hall and passes through the Reception class-room where the crosslegged class are listening to tales of long ago and far away. On the other side of the bright and busy classroom she pulls open the heavy blue door to the back hall and turns towards Year 1. Three boys clatter out of the lavatory, shoot her a brief, appalled glance and disappear across the assembly hall to their class. She notices that the floor is flooded, again. Mr Brock, already alert, passes her with a mop and bucket in hand.

Martha heads for the classroom. Doug, the teacher, is addressing the class. 'Zebras, you are going to be working with Mrs Chambers on the computers! Please pick up your worksheets and your pencils and line up by the door.' Martha waits by the door for her line of Zebras. They wrestle and push and shove towards her. 'Zebras', she calls, 'We are not going anywhere like this. Line up nicely please. Thank you Ryan, thank you Sahara. Thank you children at the back for your sensible line.' She counts under her breath. Seven Zebras. 'OK Year 1, walking quietly please!' They make the small journey to the com-puter desks and each settles to his or her task. Martha helps them to sign in, open up the document and read the worksheet of instructions. They work noisily, but they work well. A stranger appears in the doorway and slips noise-lessly into a seat in the corner. The children stare, Martha gives a nervous half-nod, half-smile and continues with her rounds. She looks back along the row of bent heads, and freezes. There were six Zebras now, where had Danu dis-appeared to? Surreptitiously she checks his normal hiding places, glancing back across the corridor to the classroom. She puts her head around the door and quickly scans the Tigers and Elephants left in the room. Doug looks up, 'Danu?' she mouths across the nodding heads, 'Not here' he assures her.

Not good timing Danu, Martha thinks as she goes back to her group, how long can I leave it before I say anything? I am going to have to own up that I have lost a child, and the longer I leave it the worse it gets! She was not, it must be said, particularly worried about Danu. He often played this game, and could come to little harm in this familiar, child safe environment. Nevertheless, a few anxious minutes pass and Martha knows that she must do something. She meets the stranger's cool gaze, and notices a small movement under the art table in the corner. The bright plastic tablecloth was swinging slightly. Now what?, thought Martha. Do I leave him there and hope she has not noticed? Do I own up and haul him out? Has she noticed and is waiting to see what I will do? Seconds pass as if they are hours, Martha can read nothing in the cool stranger's eyes. She gives nothing away. Martha takes a deep breath, raises her voice and takes a chance. She gambles on her knowledge of Danu and his tricks, and on his love of computer games; she does not want to appear silly or inefficient. 'Danu, your computer is ready here for you, and I have got your favourite activity on the screen.' There is the scrape of velcro shoes on the floor, and Danu appears, as if by magic, under the stranger's feet. He scuttles to his perch at the monitor, delighted with himself and with Martha. She spends some minutes helping him to catch up and waiting for her thudding heart rate to slow. And then slowly, she turns to look around the room. The inspector has left, satisfied. Nothing happened here today, but another story is added to the box.

> TAs need to think on their feet and make it up as they go along. Every day is different.

6

Just one more record

The DJ's cheery morning voice rudely interrupted her deep sleep. Claire reluctantly squinted at the glowing numbers on her clock, and tried to remind herself why she had thought it would be a good idea to get up earlier. An extra half hour in the morning would be so useful, it would be her time, to put some washing in and load the dishwasher, maybe fix a healthy breakfast for everyone and put her makeup on standing still instead of running out of the door. Even an extra five minutes would make a difference, and then when she got home at lunchtime she would not have to deal with the normal bombsite. There might even be time to look through those units before college. But it was still dark outside and so cold, she would just listen to the end of this record and then she really would get up. The record ended and the DJ announced another old favourite; it was still just as cold. Perhaps she would listen to just one more.

More than an hour later Claire was running and shouting. It is a well recognised fact in most homes that the minutes between 7am and 8.30 am pass more quickly than at any other time of the day, they just disappear. The children were up and dressed but only through the sheer volume and willpower of their mother, 'uniform, breakfast, teeth, shoes, book bags', she reminded them loudly. She brushed on her mascara in front of the hall mirror as she ushered them out of the door, and did her lipstick as she manoeuvred the large car down the long drive.

She eased into a space at the far end of the car park, and walked with the children to the Juniors door. Other mums greeted her in the easy, school-gate way that recognises that everyone has recently undergone a similar ordeal. She made her way to catch Jo before she left. This morning Jo was dressed for the woods, in wellies and waterproofs. Claire had noticed Jo's shaggy and excitable collie tied at the gate and thought how nice it would be to be able hike the trails through the ancient woodland opposite school this morning instead of muddling through another numeracy hour. But she pushed that thought away, only to be faced by another even less appealing image. Tonight she and Jo were on duty for the local Beavers group that they helped run. They quickly arranged who would do what, chiefly that Jo would buy or collect all the supplies that they needed for their spring bulb planting session, and Claire turned reluctantly towards school.

Wednesday was a particularly long day, Year 3 and 4 all morning; and then the raucous, unruly and irrepressible Beavers in the evening. Not for the first time, she wondered why she always said 'Yes' to things when people were asking for helpers. It seemed to be the same people who were on all the committees at school and in the village. If you want something done, ask the busiest person. Of course, she had started at school as a volunteer. A few years back, when her two were in the infants, they had asked for parents to come in and listen to readers. A few mums had jumped at the chance to see what went on in their children's classes, and she had really enjoyed it. So when a paid position came up it seemed obvious to apply. To be honest the hours and the holidays really suited her, there could not be a more ideal job that fitted around the children. She liked that she could be involved in their world even though she was at work; and if anything went wrong she was already there, not stuck in town and battling through the traffic to sort them out.

But all of this did not solve the heavy feeling in the pit of her stomach as she walked past reception and headed for her classroom. Overnight the new display in the hall had taken shape, the 3D woodland scene looked marvellous, with foxes and badgers and mice seeming to leap from the walls all along the corridor. This job could be fantastic, she thought, with just a bit more preparation and communication. She hated that feeling of not knowing what might come up next and then being asked to do something that she had not had an opportunity to think about in advance.

Yesterday, Harry had sprung a session on her with a small group of 6 children who had been trailing all week. He had just said, 'right, take them on a table with a small whiteboard and just sort of go through it with them' and she had experienced a few minutes of blind panic because she had not done anything like that before. She did not know what to say, whether they would take any notice of her, or what she would do if they messed about. And she had got nothing written down and no examples or games or anything worked out in advance. But it had been fine, it was, after all, just the same old thing they had been struggling with all week and they had all managed to complete that first stage and even write a few words by the end of the session. Perhaps it was just as well that she had not known about it in beforehand because then she could have lain awake all night worrying. No, better to be prepared she decided.

It was all a matter of good communication, it did not help that her time was shared out between various teachers so she had no 'home base', and one of them never seemed to be very sure whether she wanted to be helped or not. Claire still did not feel confident enough to take the initiative herself so each morning there was that awkward 15 minutes while she stood in the class-room, sort of waiting for the day to start and to be given something to do. There is a limit to the number of times you can tidy the book corner and craft boxes or sharpen the pencils! It is lovely to be part of a well oiled machine, she reflected, but not so nice to feel like a spare part.

Juliana had given her a brilliant idea the other day. They had been discussing their early morning start, because the beginning of the day had recently been reorganised, and Juliana had mentioned that she got on with listening to readers. She had her own list to work through; she knew who needed extra support and she organised herself so that she always had something to be getting on with. It was difficult to get through the whole list each week, Claire admitted, and this approach would mean that she could easily fit an extra 2 or 3 before registration was complete. Resolutely she made her way to the reading lists and got herself organised. Juliana was lucky to work in the same classroom with the same teacher all the time. They were like a team; both knew what the other was doing and how they worked. Sometimes it was diffi-cult to remember who the teacher was and who the assistant was in that partnership, Claire mused.

Time for reflection ended abruptly with the sound of the first bell, Class 3 started to filter in, faces glowing from the early morning chill. They scrambled for their desks and reading books and there was a smell of the open air and a small hum of voices as Harry took the register and organised dinner lists. A little self-consciously Claire called the first child on her list and asked him to begin reading. She helped him sound out new words and encouraged him to keep going and to get the sense and the humour of the story. Automatically marking the words with her finger she glanced up at Harry, searching for approval. But he was occupied with the business of the day. Claire thanked her reader and asked him to send her the next person. There was just time for one more before they rearranged themselves for the numeracy hour. Fan-tastic! It was still only 9.05 and Claire felt she had already achieved something.

Harry began his multiplication lesson, using pages on the interactive white-board. On this occasion the system worked perfectly and the magic pen revealed the answers, much to the delight of everyone. Claire watched and let her mind wander. She decided what to cook for supper and refused to think about the Beavers meeting until later. She noticed that the method for multi-plication that Harry was teaching was completely different from her own, she must remember to use his way. It would be so easy to confuse everyone.

As the children divided into groups to work in pairs Claire went to 'her' table and sat alongside them, 'does everyone know what to do?' she questioned and encouraged and checked their work. She knew exactly which two would be last to get going and who would need most of her help, sometimes it felt as if she was dragging them to keep up, squeezing answers out of them and she could see that they were bemused by the process, but at least they had some-thing written down. She used her fingers to help with counting in 2s, 'good girl', she commented, 'how did you do that?' Sometimes children from another group came for help; there was always movement between the tables. She looked at her watch, still only 9.30 – today was going to be a long day. 'Watch your '9' Chris', Claire warned, 'you've done it the wrong way around again – yeah, there we go'.

The clock crept around to 10.00 and Claire started to mark answers, and to help the children who had not finished. Finally it was time for assembly. As the children wound their way down the stairs, she wiped whiteboards, col-lected up markers and erasers and tidied up the tables and chairs. Juliana appeared with a mop and a bucket, having cleared up an 'accident' in her classroom. 'Ready for a coffee?' she called, 'there might even be some biscuits left if we go now'.

Later that week, several literacy hours and committee meetings later and after a triumphant bulb planting session with the Beavers, Claire was doing her lipstick again as she got into the car. There was just time to drive the 15 miles into town and park at college for the afternoon. She had been delighted when the headteacher had agreed to pay for her NVQ3 course and, despite initial misgivings and nerves she was really, really enjoying it.

This time last year she complained that she had not even done the four week Induction Course yet and now look, here she was committed to the NVQ. Of course, there was not really time in her week to fit it in and sometimes the pile of coursework sat in the corner of the room and made her feel bad and stressed and guilty. Most days passed in a blur and she often felt like she was only just keeping all the plates spinning, or all the balls in the air, or whatever the phrase was. But she was mostly keeping on top of it and she was determined to finish in the minimum time allowed. Her tutor had said that if they really pressed on they could do it in six months. It was certainly helpful. It was interesting to see how she fitted into the criteria. Gathering the witness statements made her think about what she was actually doing in the classroom and the sessions at college made her realise that there is plenty to learn and loads of resources to help her learn. It would be good to have something to show on paper at the end of it all, she thought to herself as she found a space in the college car park. She listened to the end of the record on the radio, and went in.

> TAs need to be professionally managed.
> They need careful deployment, clear
> instructions and authentic tasks.

7

A Class Act

'Don't let him be there yet ... oh, please don't let him be there yet!' Juliana forces her car through the morning traffic as quickly as safety allows. One red light or snarl up caused by someone else's thoughtless parking is all it takes to throw out her careful timetable. She has to leave the house by 8.37. So important is this timeslot that the clock in the kitchen is deliberately set fast, just to make sure. She passes the car park of the village shop and post office and crawls up the hill towards the gates.

The footpath is a mass of straggling families and bikes and dogs, all facing that basic challenge: getting to school on time. Mothers and fathers drag toddlers behind them or push babies in buggies as they accompany their older children to school. The uniform fleeces and sweaters are jewel bright in the dull morning light. The children grip their lunchboxes and book bags tightly; some are bringing precious treasures to show. Some jolly families are reciting tables or testing spellings on the way. Other children are crying and dragging their feet. Cars pass with children from further away, or those who got up too late to walk. Early birds have bagged the spaces nearest to the school gates and the mothers are sitting and ticking off the reading records as their children struggle with their reading and their counterparts struggle up the hill. Small groups of boys and girls link up and make their own way up; these mothers meet up to talk, to laugh, to gossip. It is a supportive network centred on the large and friendly village and the school is an important fixed point for them all.

Juliana used to be one of the mums in the playground. Her easy smile and friendly nature put her at the centre of all that was going on. But now her morning challenge is different. She needs to get through the school gates and into the staff car park before Mr Fox puts out the traffic cones and blocks her entrance! A scowl from the caretaker, and knowing that he knows how late she is, yet again, can ruin the day. She turns up the drive and breathes a relieved sigh; the way is clear, she zips past the caretaker's neat house and quickly parks. Her own children, who ate their breakfast at home, pick up their own lunch boxes and PE kit and scramble out. They go by different entrances to start their days.

Juliana is taking Class 3's register by the time Jess arrives. 'I'm sorry to interrupt you Mrs Rose but I have just walked through our cloakroom, and I really don't like what I see. Can I ask you to bring up everything that is on the floor?' Jess takes over registration, but Juliana is soon back with a mountain of sweaters, book bags, bits of PE kit lunch and snack boxes. 'I can't believe what I have found Miss Dove – look at all these things – whose is this? And these? Where should they be? Right, go and do it please. Class 3 you are lucky to have so many lovely things but you must learn to look after them properly. The whole school walks past our cloakroom and ours is the worst in the school. We need everyone to try harder, do you agree Miss Dove?'

Juliana returns to the register and the lunch list while Jess attends to a crying child and hands out the whiteboards. The children are reading and there is a gentle hum of chatter, until Juliana instructs, 'Lips away now please everyone'.

The morning begins with maths, everyone is on the carpet listening to Jess' explanation for doubling and halving numbers, 'that was tricky, guys!' she says as they work through a complicated example. Unfortunately some children are drawing on their whiteboards or talking to their friends or just staring into space. These are mostly gathered around Juliana's feet – she encourages and supports and gives a gentle commentary. Ryan thinks he knows the answer to a question, he looks urgently at Juliana and mouths his response, she gives him an encouraging nod and he feels bold enough to put his hand up and answer. Everyone is impressed. Juliana tags the dreamers and the wigglers, already knowing who has 'got it' and who has not. She uses her hands to illustrate and rephrases questions to help them keep up.

When the class divides into groups Juliana stays with her children, using her small white board to explain what she is doing. The first task is to write the short date, but precious minutes are lost waiting for everyone to settle down and find what they need for the lesson. They all need lots of support. Elsewhere the other children, the self-starters, are whizzing through the number problems. But Juliana is still coaxing the date out of reluctantly held pencils. She draws Jess aside and mentions that they will not manage to achieve the whole of the set task. Jess nods in assent, 'see how they go today and you decide whether they can move on tomorrow'. Juliana grabs a tray of coloured cubes and improvises a demonstration of the basic concept. The children watch bemused and slowly count the halved towers of cubes. She works her way around the group, everyone has put something, she awards a star for the best work and then she collects in the books. It is time to line up for assembly. As the children file out Jess and Juliana discuss the group and the children, they alter their plans for the rest of the week to allow for the slower progress.

During assembly they work together on a wall display, chatting easily about their lives, their work, the recent staff meeting and the literacy hour they are teaching after break. They look through the books together, pointing out tiny breakthroughs and achievements and stumbling blocks. They assess progress as they go, making adjustments to their plans and fine tuning. The tacit understanding between them means that there is much that does not need to be said. They are in tune, they have a shared vocabulary of classroom language and terminology which the children understand and respond to. They turn to each other for support in the classroom and present a united front, it is a class act.

The bell rings for the end of assembly and the children tip out onto the playground to play. Jess and Juliana move off together for their own break. One of them puts the kettle on and reaches for the jar of coffee; the other raids the fridge and the biscuit tin. Jess notices Juliana's new skirt, 'I love it, is that the one we were looking at? It really suits you!' Juliana has a dancer's body and she moves with grace, every movement balanced and centred. Her careful clothes, hair and makeup match those of her classroom friend and colleague. This autumn they wear knee-length skirts with opaque tights and heeled boots with pointy toes; their tops are layered and fitted. They are well polished, well heeled and well co-ordinated.

'Thanks!' she sips her coffee and forces her mind from fashion to maths – how can she show doubling and halving so that the children grasp the concept? She fusses with the loose ends of her hair which are twisted and stabbed into place with a wooden pin; she thinks about Ryan – when he was handling the blocks he suddenly seemed to make the connection she was hoping for. It was one of the lovely moments that make the job, and that morning scramble, worthwhile.

They sit with their coffee and biscuits in comfortable silence. The windows of the warm room steam up as more staff trickle in and make use of the kettle and toaster. Jess leaves as the bell rings and Juliana makes her way to the classroom. She puts out pencil pots and literacy books and Jess soon returns with Class 3 in tow. They noisily take their places on the carpet but quickly settle down, 'lips away everybody'! Juliana writes the aim of the lesson on the board while Jess begins her explanation. Then she settles with her group again, asking them questions and keeping them focused.

The children work quietly in their groups; Jess and Juliana make the rounds prompting and helping and answering questions. The children are quiet and purposeful, some are highlighting the pronouns in a text others are writing sentences and replacing nouns with pronouns. Juliana makes up examples as she needs them, checking all the time that the children know why they are doing what they are doing. This is the best kind of lesson. The children are working hard and the classroom is tranquil. Playtime must have been perfect, they have used lots of energy.

As the literacy hour draws to a close, Jess prepares to take the class next door to watch a video and Juliana collects up books. She looks through the work her groups have produced during the morning and makes little notes to bring up in their team planning meeting this afternoon. She knows and understands what the children can achieve, who is likely to have problems, who has recently made progress.

As the bell rings again for lunch Juliana and Jess meet up for sandwiches and more coffee and to make plans for the rest of the week. It is a satisfying process, pleasing to feel well prepared and in command of the material.

As she drives home at the end of the day Juliana reflects on her job and how much she enjoys working with the children and being a member of a team. She had not planned this career for herself. When she left school she had no idea that she would end up back in the classroom. She had imagined a life as a ballet teacher, but when that had not worked out she had quickly found herself a Youth Training Scheme placement; it was either that or you were 'on the pots' in this area of the midlands – and she definitely did not want to work in a factory again. She had spent some years as a sales representative for various car dealerships. That had been quite glamorous really and she loved meeting and greeting people. But when she stopped to have the children she had not missed the work, although the money had been nice.

Now she was back at school herself. The school was funding her one evening a week Foundation Degree course. She had to write essays, reflect on her practice and compile a portfolio of competences. She was enjoying all the reading and found it helpful in the classroom. Who knew where it might all end?

As they arrive home she is brought back to earth with a crash. The remains of their hasty breakfast still lies on the table, there was no time to pick up pyjamas and wet towels or coffee cups and cereal bowls, there never is. The evening routine must start with picking up the morning; there is homework to supervise and something (who knows what at this stage) to make for supper. And then it will be time to repack the lunch boxes and the PE kits and make sure everyone has clean outfits for the morning.

Juliana sighs as she notices the pile of reading on the floor. She has not had time to prepare for this week's class. Doubling and halving and pronouns are pushed from her mind as she sets to the tasks in hand. She glances at the kitchen clock and reminds herself that it is not really quite that late. But in no time at all those hands will be rushing towards 8.37 again and she will be desperately hoping she can outrun Mr Fox for the second day running.

Today was a good day.

> When teacher and TA work together as a team the teaching and learning improves and standards go up.

8

Magic at the manor

The vast hall sits at ease, enfolded in a thousand acres of parkland. The wide square façade, adorned with flaring columns and generous rectangles of window, is pinkish in the dawning sunshine. A mirror hard lake reflects a glinting image. Daring and secret stories of history and mystery wait to be discovered. Everything is in order and cherished. Behind a geometry of brick walls there are cottage gardens for cutting and kitchen gardens for produce. There is a home farm with pigs and cattle and hens, but the silent ones inside the mansion do not get their hands dirty. An army of servants work all the daylight hours to keep the fires alight, the water hot and the ovens full. There is a laundry and a school room and a carriage hall as well as state rooms fit for a queen.

It is 1871. Life is hard for the men and women who live in the draughty spaces of the hall and who rise in the dark to start the day. Mrs Stern marches towards her domain, as she does every day, to coax the vast black range into life and set the huge boiling coppers in place. Her voice is sharp and her manner tough, but she softens as she sees the new recruits waiting in a neat line outside her kitchen. They wait in silence, eyes huge and faces pale. They are excited and nervous. They have no idea what to expect. They have to be recruited into the ways and manners of the kitchen staff. They need to learn to speak only when spoken to, to work hard and to obey immediately. She lifts a heavy key from the chain about her waist and opens the solid doors. She straightens her mop cap and indicates that the children should follow her inside. They gaze at their surroundings. An oak table dominates the room, shoulder high to them; it is larger than any table they have ever seen. The cooking range is in an arched and tiled recess that occupies the entire far wall, directly in front of them wooden shelves disappear to the roof, lined with gleaming copper pans and dishes and moulds.

The children shuffle and poke and risk a soft giggle but Mrs Stern turns on them with a no-nonsense eye. They look anxiously at me, wanting to know how to be. Mrs Stern starts to talk to them about the morning ahead, what they must do and how they must act. She tells them about the family in the dining room, biscuits that must be cooked for tea and the marzipan fancies to be crafted ready for a fine banquet later. She talks about precious ingredients that have come from afar, exotic lemons and almonds, spices and sugar kept in tightly stoppered flasks; butter from the herd and flour from the mill. She explains how everything must be made from scratch, produced themselves. They catch the sense of far off lives. But most of all she talks of cleanliness. They hold out their hands for inspection and she shakes her head and tuts aloud. They scrub their hands in a deep ceramic sink and she hands out their uniform. I help them into unfamiliar garments, working smocks and aprons and little caps to cover their hair. We tie up laces and smile at our strange reflections.

The group is divided up and assigned tasks, manual tasks with strange equipment; hard repetitive tasks that reflect hard, repetitive lives. They sweep and polish the floor, wipe the range and scrub the draining boards. They dust the shelves and I circulate to each group. I help them to understand what they are doing. I check that they are having fun, learning, listening, experiencing. I remind them of the history and science we have done in preparation for this. I remind them to behave and to be polite. Mrs Stern judges the moment to perfection and just as they begin to tire and lose interest, she calls them all to the table.

They crowd around the edge and help in the weighing and combining of ingredients. The large ceramic mixing bowl is passed round and each child takes part in the process until a tray of homely biscuits is ready for the range. A pair of lads is assigned to watch the fires and I keep them in view, willing them not to play the fool, not to touch anything, break anything, hurt themselves. A large timer is placed on the table and the children keep solemn eyes on the running grains of sand as the air fills with spice and sugar. Mrs Stern is already moving on, busy about her morning ritual, mindful of the demands of her important role. Marzipan, so very precious, is passed around and the children mould its jewel bright colours into tiny pears and bananas and strawberries. She is critical of their efforts and strident in her call for perfection. Someone at the end of the table looks close to tears, overwhelmed suddenly by the strangeness and riskiness of her situation. I take my place alongside her, a familiar face to share the burden and beat the fear. We work together in near-silence, listening to Mrs Stern as she talks about the family and their life. The children warm to the topic and risk questions and comment; she is generous with her knowledge, encouraging them to think and to be inquisitive. The sand runs out of the glass and the children call out. They gather around the range as Mrs Stern opens the door and brings the biscuits to the table; one for each child, warm wrapped in crinkly paper and smelling good. I record the moment with the school camera, catching colourful moments for our memory bank, already planning the display of the day. They peel off their layers of clothes and I remind them to hang them at the door, to shake hands with Mrs Stern and to say thank you. They leave clutching their precious snack and I walk slowly around the great kitchen checking for lost property before joining them in the sunny square.

There is time, a few minutes, to eat our biscuits and talk about what we have seen and done, before another figure appears. The children again shift and nudge and giggle, but Mr Dour is an imposing figure with a long black coat and high frilly collar. He views the straggly line before him with disdain and stalks into the house. We follow, subdued. We are greeted by Annie, who hands out school uniform: overdresses for the girls, waistcoats and caps for the boys and we line up in strict order. Mr Dour wants the girls at the front. Annie hands each child a Victorian penny with which they have to pay for their day at school. The children turn worried faces towards me, I follow them picking up dropped caps and lost pennies. They pay their dues and sit tightly, waiting for the register.

The small wooden desks are arranged in rows, with backless benches pulled close. There are high windows and high ceilings but the classroom is a dark and colourless place. Some faded maps adorn the walls. Mr Dour is very strict for the first fifteen minutes and they learn to sit up straight, to answer quickly and politely and to resist the urge to chat. They learn that children must remain silent. He quizzes them on their times tables and general knowledge, quickly identifying a rogue to put in the corner. He checks their handwriting next and they practice writing on small slates, squeaking the chalk in untidy loops as they copy unfamiliar and adult text. They turn to me for help and reassurance until they begin to relax and join in the fun. They are fascinated and horrified as they listen to tales of strictly controlled, uncomfortable young lives and crane forward to look at the array of canes that Mr Dour flexes for them. They hear about lessons, holidays and festivals, some even begin to consider school attendance as a privilege. A bell tolls in the distance and we are released into the sunshine again.

Year 4 has a lot to say as we sit at the picnic tables and eat our lunch. I help with lunch boxes and containers, ripping open a dozen tricky drinks cartons and handing out apples and crisps. I keep them at the tables and check that every-one has eaten something and then encourage them to gather up the debris. Gradually other groups join us from different parts of the house and we share experiences and find out who else fell foul of Mrs Stern and Mr Dour. Off the rein at last and unfettered by Victorian ghosts, our Year 4 plays in the sunshine. They re-enact their favourite scenes and themes, they run hard and fast over the neatly trimmed grass; they rejoice in being seen and heard, aware perhaps for the first time that such freedom is to be cherished. I talk to Miss Finch over the water bottles. We sit for a few minutes watching the scene, enjoying the fresh air, counting heads, vigilant for safety, planning the next stage.

A distant bell summons us back to the 19th Century and we gather up our groups, count heads, organise pairs and snake back up to the big house. All together we follow our guide on a tour of other realms. Miss Finch and I monitor the children, encouraging them to keep up, rounding up stragglers and ensuring compliant behaviour. We hand out trail maps and pencils and help them to notice interesting features: furniture we have seen in books; cos-tumes and customs we have talked about; methods of transport; traditional toys and tools. We question and point out, we chivvy and restrain, we listen and absorb and stay alert. We make our weary way to the home farm to look at the animals and meet the Miller and his wife but by now our attention is waning and so is our energy. It has been a long day. Small legs begin to trail behind, children hang back to hold my hands when earlier they were racing ahead. We spy our bus creeping towards us between the meadows by the river. We are ready to leave the 19th Century behind but one final trial awaits us: the 21st Century gift shop! Year 4 brighten and find new energy as we approach. Wearily we organise them into small groups, agree our policy about sweeties (no big bags allowed) and I take the first group in. They wander bemused past the shelves of gorgeous educational books and make their way to the counter of pocket money toys. I watch them carefully work out how far their coins will stretch and make their choices. They all want to buy the same bits and pieces, some also look for gifts for mums and dads. They should all be armed with the same, modest, amount of spending money but I check carefully to make sure that no one is embarrassed or heartbroken, helping them to count their change and make sensible decisions. I decide rapidly to ban the range of cheap noisemakers and instruments that some are drawn to, and counsel against things that look dangerous or not robust enough to last the journey home.

At last we are done and all the money is spent. They clamber back onto the bus clutching sealed paper bags of treasures; we climb aboard clutching first aid kit, cameras and worksheets. We count heads as we climb the steps and we count heads again as they sit down and buckle up, we check seat belts and poor travellers, we say our thanks and wave goodbye. Weary Year 4 start to sing but soon slump into sleep; lulled by the hum of traffic, the warmth of the bus and the scent of crushed apples. Nobody is sick. They rally as they recognise the approach to school. We help them gather up their bags and coats and jump down into waiting arms. I check off each child and watch them leave with people that I recognise. I overhear snippets of conversation as they leave, excited chatter about childhoods long ago.

We make our way into school to return the kit. It is 4.30 and even the after school clubs have finished. I meet the Deputy Head in the hall, 'how was the Manor?' he asks, 'Cool', I reply, 'it wove its magic as usual, the children always love it'. Since he is there I ask him what I should do about the extra hours I have worked. Can I put in for a full day, or take a half day off in lieu?

His reply chases the magic from the day, 'well, trips are a bit of a grey area really, you do not get paid, you are like a parent-helper, you are enjoying yourself!'

Grey areas suggest a lack of respect or a lack of care.
Think carefully about the practical issues such as
overtime and payment for trips.

9

I don't think about school too much

Bright, brittle November sunlight shines through the parchment-coloured vertical blind that covers the windows. Some of it has fallen down and here a low shaft of light pierces the room, briefly blinding everyone in its trajectory. Ellie, teaching assistant in this joint year 5 and 6 class is thinking about the day ahead, and about the times she has spent in this oh-so familiar school.

These upstairs classrooms are nearly all windows, with vast glass walls that make us feel as if we are in a large private bubble. On cold days the windows soon become steamy and opaque and on foggy autumn mornings and dark December afternoons the outside world seems to close in around us as we sit up here, lights blazing. In the summer our bubble becomes so hot that we throw open all the windows and enjoy the breezes that sing in the pines; although the wasps always seem to know when the fruit is handed out. Actually, I think primary classrooms are very much like bubbles. The outside world goes on as always, all the everyday things happen: the days of the week pass; the seasons change; and school has its own exclusive routine. And you have to leave your own 'out of the bubble' life outside. It does not really matter what is going on out there, in here 'bubble life' remains at a constant pitch. Not that I think too much about school if I am honest, it does not make a lot of difference to me really, not once I am out of the bubble.

Right – what and who have we got today, and what day is it? Fine, this lot are fine. Of course they are a bit noisy, like all ten year olds, and I do not like being drowned out. I like a nice quiet classroom. But these are a good bunch. First, however, I have got Joel. He is doing really well with these reading exercises. I had my doubts at first because they are just pages and pages of sounds and groups of letters – nonsense words. But they are making a difference to the way he approaches his reading. I can see it happening. For the first time he seems to be reading what is on the page rather than what he thinks is on the page. We whizz through them, I mark the place with my finger and we can move on only if he does a complete page perfectly. It is amazing how quickly you get to check and amend automatically. Of course, I have always got my eye on the clock and on the other children clattering into the room, but I think that the rhythm and the routine of doing five minutes with me every morning is useful. And it is great to see him making progress. Those kind of things really do make it worthwhile here; the little triumphs and successes; the 'Oh, I get it!' moment. When they get their results you know that you have made a difference.

It is also nice to have something to be getting on with first thing in the morning. I know Claire and Jenny both feel a bit under used first thing, and there is nothing worse than feeling that you are wasting your time, or are not really needed. I like to know what I am doing next and what is going to come up during the day, I am not too keen on surprises. Some people thrive on un-certainty, but I would say most of us like to feel at least a bit prepared.

I can just note Joel's scores in the book while the class is changing around and moving into their numeracy groups. Things are a bit different here because we have four year 5 and 6 classes, so we can divide the whole lot into four groups and run a different numeracy or literacy task in each classroom. Everyone here, and they are nearly all here now, is working on the same task. That means I do not have a particular group to concentrate on. I am free to help wherever. Once Mark has done his explanation we both move around and answer questions and mark work; although I have noticed that I move around the class while he stays at his desk and they take their work to him. I wonder why that is? It's a bit hard on the knees actually, constantly up and down beside these low chairs and tables!

Today we are looking at 2D shapes, it is very basic stuff. They all have a work-sheet of measurements to finish and later I will stick them in their maths books. After Christmas we can look at these and decide which of the Year 6s need to come to my booster maths classes. I can not believe how quickly they come around each year. Time flies in school.

- Think about it carefully Hayley, what do you need to find out? And if these two sides are the same and those two sides are the same what does that make altogether?
- What are you going to do first?

- Each one is seven so what have you got altogether?
- John look, these two sides are the same.
- Yes Joel, what have you got altogether?
- What does that make?
- Yes, altogether
- ... altogether?
- ... what does it make?
- Who has not got a ruler? Why not? Well go and fetch it then.
- Of course you need it
- JOHN ... !

What is it about little boys and cartridge pens? How can there be so much ink from one small cartridge? Oh and look at his shirt ... and his face!

Thankfully Mark is starting his round up session so I have time to clear this up before it gets traipsed all around the classroom. 'John, just move into that seat please, no, actually better wash your hands and face first. Don't fuss just do it.'

Break at last and I am dying for a coffee. Gosh, Jill is still working on that display board in the main corridor. She has made a fantastic job of it, those sparkly fishes and sea creatures look great with the wavy fronds of netting and fabric over the top, really effective. I am always looking for good ideas, I might use that spangled look in our room. Every spare minute we seem to be stapling and sticking and making things so that the children's work is displayed nicely.

Marvelous, someone has put the kettle on already and that toast smells good. Our staff room is a friendly place really, we all get on and today everyone is in high spirits for some reason, there is lots of teasing and laughter. At the moment we are choosing books from the Christmas catalogue before the rep comes back on Friday, it is good to get a bit of early shopping done! I do love Christmas in school, especially helping to produce the Christmas production. It is a highlight of the year and always worth the costume dramas, props nightmares and sleepless nights from half term onwards. The children love it of course, and so do the parents.

Not that I have had much information about Christmas arrangements yet. Do not get me started! We are a happy team, and the job suits me perfectly, especially the holidays. I could not bear to be without the holidays now. But I would say that communication could be better, it is hard to get information about anything; from training courses to overtime. We always seem to be in the dark about what is happening and what plans have been made for the future. I know we could attend the weekly staff meeting, although I am not sure everyone would welcome us. But, to be honest, we do not get paid for that time, and 80 per cent of the material is nothing to do with us, so why would we opt to attend? But a ten minute slot some other time, just to share information from on high would be helpful. For example, it was the last week of term before we found out what classes and hours we would be getting in September. Actually nothing much had changed, but that is not the point; we did not know this until it was confirmed. Teachers would not put up with that so I am not sure we should. Perhaps I will have a word ...

Break passes too quickly and it is on to literacy work now. Again, we have just got one group in here and we are looking at the difference between autobiography and biography. Mark is giving his explanation and I can just organise these maths books while I keep an eye on the class. If someone is wriggling it is usually enough for them to see me watching them. But I think I might just move a bit closer to John, 'what are the key points we are looking for, John?' Today they have to study a text, decide whether it is biography or autobiography, and then write a précis.

- Come on Kim, we are going to get some work done today, we are actually going to get something done.
- Have you started yet John?
- Let's have a look, where have you got to?
- What are you going to do first?
- Where are your key points ... so therefore is it biography?
- Why not?
- ... Why?
- John, do it in pencil.
- You need to see what kind of writing it is first, before you try and summarise it
- Bring me your spelling book then, right, what does it start with?
- Now listen to me, just get on.
- You really need to be moving on to your summary now.

Nobody seems to have got much done at all today, and yet we did not think this was going to be a particularly tough task. I wonder why they have not engaged with it. They are just not concentrating, and they are asking what they should be doing all the time and waiting for me to get them started. There is only five minutes left. That is interesting – another one not using capital letters for proper nouns. I had better mention it to Mark and he can remind them of the rule ... again!

Tidy up time – at last, phew! That was like getting blood out of a stone. Some days are like that.

It is nice to be leaving the bubble for today. I do not need to think about it again until tomorrow. Right, what shall we have for tea?

A TA assists. Think about what children do in school – your role will be to help them.

10

Notes on an observation

Setting: This is a tiny, tiny school, in a chocolate box village in the far north-western corner of Staffordshire. Its catchment area comprises farming families, many of whom have owned and worked this land for generations. They are organically connected to each other and the place. Their ancestors rest in the turf alongside the school. It shares a large, prominent plot with an ancient and beautiful Anglican church. Myth and legend from the Wars of the Roses wreathe around its tower and bloodied ghosts from the battlefield skulk.

The school occupies a new building with blue carpets and cream walls and huge picture windows. It has just two classes: Infants and Juniors, in literacy and mathematics lessons classes are often divided vertically by ability rather than age.

The atmosphere is positive, quiet and purposeful. It is a happy working environment. Wall displays include: using the numberline for subtraction and addition; habitats and wildlife around school; fractions, decimals and percentages; calculator keys, step by step guide to solving problems; numerical symbols; time line; artistic collage; length, capacity, time and mass.

Time and Date: 0930, Wednesday, 24 May, 2006

Present: Deborah (TA); Celia (Researcher); Classroom Teacher

Researcher's notes: We are in the Junior Classroom – all Key Stage 2 are together.

24 children in total.

After a rainy start the sun is shining, the grass has been cut recently, we can already smell lunch cooking.

No coughs or colds.

0930 Met by Deborah and introduced to staff.

Teacher (T) introduces me to class and explains, just here to speak to Mrs K and watch us!

Normal class resumes.

0945 T addresses whole class.

Deborah hovers – listening to T, answers query.

Children working in whole group – work was started yesterday in Literacy Hour (LH).

Class working independently on writing task from *Peter and the Wolf*.

Deborah working with individual child – setting up task on computer

Deborah targets 'her' group of children – checks progress.

T reminds children to think about newspaper layout, shows good examples.

0955 'Headline needs to stand out', Deborah reminds.

T stays at one table, Deborah moves around room.

Deborah record keeping (with register/clipboard/ticklist).

A word to another table, 'keep concentrating'.

Checks boy on computer.

Answers question from girl on Table 1.

Lots of hands raised, Deborah goes from hand to hand.

Kneels by each child.

Boy on computer helps himself to inhaler, Deborah monitors.

Children get up to find atlases and dictionaries etc.

1005 T working with same group, sometimes addresses whole class.

Deborah is looking through reading records, also monitoring progress of class work.

T now moving around class.

Deborah helps with a spelling, 'no difference in the sound so we have to learn the rule'.

T and Deborah circulating and correcting.

Deborah returns to boy on computer – keeps him on task.

Lady from kitchen puts head around door with query – Deborah deals with it.

1015 Deborah sorting reading records, children on task, some talking, but working independently – not a lot of teacher talk from T or Deborah.

T and Deborah spend time with each child who puts a hand up.

Deborah searches in cupboards (neat, tidy cupboards).

T-Deborah two minute discussion about an IEP, Deborah has a sheet of marks, T has another piece of information to add to the picture, 'ah, right, that's interesting'

Deborah back to boy on computer.

Noise levels rising slightly.

1025 Deborah leaves with something for the office.

Returns, smiles all the time.

'Come on, we need more than that'.

Another conference with T.

Sorting folders and papers.

'Two minutes to break, you should be checking your criteria sheets'

A child feels unwell, goes to Deborah. 'Have you had some medicine at home?'

Deborah beginning to sort resources and sheets for next class.

Calls across to boy on computer.

1030 Children line up and file out for break.

Deborah, 'Be sensible, keep out of the puddles!'

Deborah and I depart for tiny staff room. We make tea and cook brings plate of hot buttered toast.

Banter and laughter.

Chat about diets – who can eat what?

Staff in and out all the time.

Our T on playground duty – someone takes her a hot chocolate drink.

1050 After break Deborah settles Year 3 children to work individually on computers.

She gives Blue group a numeracy sheet to work on, they sit quietly waiting for her.

Deborah visits each computer – helps children to start.

1100 Deborah takes Blue group (6 children, Year 4) into empty hall for mental maths – revise basic fractions.

Others (Years 5 and 6) are having whole class numeracy lesson (equivalent fractions) with T in classroom.

Children sit on benches in vee formation; Deborah sits on chair facing them, uses easel and paper.

Practising times tables.

Takes feedback from sheets.

Monitors and checks, 'How did you get that?', 'How did you work it out?', 'How can I prove that?'

Children check their own work.

Deborah – 'Tell me what a fraction is?'

Explains, 'A fraction is something that is not a whole thing; a piece of something'.

'We have been finding fractions of things, now we are going to find fractions of numbers!'

Children groan.

Explaining, questioning, monitoring, 'Are you alright with that?'

1120 Child comes with message, T is ready for us to rejoin them.

Children wait for Deborah to finish, she gives them permission to return to classroom.

Blue group then go to work with T on carpet.

Deborah supervises the others who have been with T for first part of lesson.

Deborah works at tables with small groups.

1130 Answers questions.

Asks questions and checks understanding.

Moves around table, visits each child.

Clarifies and explains.

Monitors understanding.

1150 Checks on progress.

Has everyone finished?

Did anyone get stuck?

Does anyone need more time?

'How do you think you did?'

'How did you get on with that today?'

Feedback to T.

Collecting in work.

Encouraging packing away and getting ready for lunch.

1200 It is lunch time.

> Minute by minute, this is what it feels like to
> assist in the classroom.

11

The wrong shoes

The children breathe like dragons in the frosted morning, stamping their feet against the cold. The sunlight is crystal hard through the pointing pines, but the beauty of the morning is lost on Lois, who listens distractedly to the easy chatter at the school gate. The children file in and she waves goodbye and then moves reluctantly to the staff entrance, trying to keep her new, pinchy shoes off the grass.

She had been overjoyed to be offered the TA position last term. It allowed her to keep other commitments, offered the chance to contribute to school life and to explore a new career by working with experienced others. She was positive and energetic and excited. But the reality was so hard. From her first day she had been playing 'catch-up', everyone else was too overstretched and busy to answer her questions. There was no Induction Course because, as a parent, she was treated as an insider, but it would have been nice to know where the staff hung their coats, left their bags and went to the loo. And there was no formal introduction or announcement about her, so most people thought she was there as a helpful mum. To be included on staff bulletins and circulars, and even the tea and biscuit rota, would have made her feel part of the team. Teamwork had been a key phrase during her interview. It was in the classroom that she felt completely at sea.

For some hours each day she was the dedicated support for a charming autistic boy who needed some help with his handwriting and organisation skills. Sometimes she acted as a scribe for him during classwork periods. At other times she helped to reframe some of the confusion of the day and helped him to access the information that everyone else decoded so easily. She learned to read his atrocious writing and to understand the way that he processed information on the page.

They developed a close working relationship but she realised that she lacked specialist knowledge and had no idea what resources were available. There was no time to ask anyone. She muddled through, drawing heavily on common sense and using the Internet for ideas. She read all she could about the autism spectrum and gradually built up her skills and understanding. The rest of the time she worked with small groups in a variety of activities, and found, by inference and deduction, the things she needed to do. But not knowing what was going to happen next left her permanently disadvantaged, edgy and worried. She felt depressed and exhausted by her work and began to dread Monday mornings. She knew she was not doing a good job; she needed time to reflect on the aims and material for the day and to prepare what she was going to say and do. And there was no escaping the fact that a bit of revision of the relevant numeracy or literacy rules and skills would help her to interact more confidently and effectively.

As she makes her way to the classroom she remembers why she wanted to work here. Primary schools are wonderful, vibrant places. The glorious displays show the range of subjects covered each term. Accounts of science experiments compete for position alongside stories, poetry, 3D maths models, news from nature walks and timelines. Fragile artwork is carefully displayed and ready to be taken home; projects are colourful and thoughtful and mounted proudly. Lists of prompts for good writing, better behaviour and number rules paper the walls, along with book reports and news. The warm, welcoming environment begins to unlock the chill from the playground. But in class the children are already lining up, still wearing their coats and boots. 'Off we go to the bus Mrs Jennings', says the classroom teacher as they trail past. Lois falls into line and is dismayed to learn they have a half-day traffic survey ahead of them. Everyone else is noisy and cheery. Everyone else is warmly dressed. No one else is trying out pinching shoes.

At lunchtime, shattered, frozen and in agony she checks belts and buckles and drops into the last remaining seat on the returning bus. 'How's it going?' Jan, another TA, is sitting next to her. Lois confesses that she did not know about the trip and Jan looks genuinely concerned: 'was it on your plans?' Lois had asked about plans once but had been told firmly that they were the personal work of the teacher, and not to be touched by anyone else. Lois is loyal and diplomatic, but it is clear that Jan's experience is very different. She has a regular planning session with her teacher, when they discuss learning objectives and how her input can contribute; the weekly plans and long-term goals are posted on the wall. Curriculum folders and other professional resources are available in a shared cupboard. Jan says that last term she would have been really caught out without a plan as she was in charge of pancake making for the whole of Year 2. 'There's no way I could have done it without consulting Nigella in advance!'. Jan appears confident, focused and in control. She is part of the team.

Lois notices the beautiful day for the first time and, as she relaxes back in the bus and kicks off the unsuitable shoes, she sees clearly what she needs to ask for. She sees that it is not too much to expect advance information about the day. She recognises that she would like to be involved in planning. She also recognises that she must ask for appropriate training and support. She realises that she need never wear the wrong shoes again.

> TAs need time to plan and prepare for the activities ahead. They will do a better job if they know in advance what they are doing and why.

12

We hate our jobs but we love what we do!

'Felix, put that rock down, love', Rachel called calmly as she moved swiftly to diffuse a minor flashpoint between a cowboy and an exotic dancer. It was a beautiful early summer afternoon and the garden was warm and lush. Some children were sitting under the pergola finishing their art, absolutely the last chance before it was all mounted; others were choosing their activities. There were quoits in one corner and some huge alphabet building tiles as well as the ever popular sand box, dressing up and puppet theatre. The warm sunshine was making everyone mellow and there was remarkably little dispute over territory.

Rachel and Martha patrolled the groups, moving people on, settling small squabbles, encouraging good manners and helping to do up and undo costumes. Unexpectedly, a father arrived to take his daughter to the dentist. Rachel took him into school to check the paperwork. She returned shortly with a large box of cherry tomatoes. It was Healthy School Week and so there were yummy tomatoes for snack time. She handed them out and talked about how delicious and full-of-vitamins they were. All the children tried them, many scrambled to claim seconds and Rachel talked to them about sharing.

As she sat back and watched the children playing, Rachel remembered how hard they had had to battle for the privilege of leading these sessions. Teachers were going to be given planning time away from their classes and the head-teacher was going to hire supply cover. Rachel and Martha had put together an offer which meant that they would run structured play sessions for the whole school and share the extra money that would have gone to the supply teacher. They emphasised how valuable it would be because the children would get continuity as she and Martha already knew them all.

Rachel was protective of her tasks, she was pleased that she could do them well and did not want anyone taking them over. She also realised that in such a small school she and Martha probably had much more scope for enlarging their areas of responsibility and carving out an interesting niche than other teaching assistants did. And she knew that they formed a formidable pair. It was amazing to find a soulmate on such a small team, someone who had shared similar experiences – they were really lucky to have each other. The teachers were initially dubious about whether she and Martha could manage the sessions and even queried what they thought they could do. But they had fought their corner well and had proved, in the last four months, that they were more than equal to the task. Structured play ran like a dream and they loved the challenge of keeping it relevant to other areas of the curriculum as well as fun and full of variety.

Rachel was brought back to reality by an indignant howl from the sandbox. Someone had dumped all the sand onto the blanket. She cleared up the mess, carefully tipping the sand back, and smilingly banished the suspects to another part of the garden. This was why she loved the job, there was always something different happening when you worked with children, she mused, and it was often very funny. She winced as she remembered Joe refusing to come out from under the table just when she had sole charge of Year 1 and Year 2 before lunch; or that time that Martha had 'lost' one of her Zebra group as the Ofsted Inspector walked through the door. Martha was still supervising the artists so she continued with her patrol, dragging Adam and Jane out from behind the playhouse where they were locked in an inappropriate clinch, and joining in the audience for an improvised puppet show.

As she sat beside the children in the sunshine the smell of the essential oils being released from the garden plants and herbs tugged at the edges of her memory and she was transported to another time and another place. Another life.

The traffic noise from the road below the playground changed in tone and vigour. It became more raucous and urgent. There was the sound of ancient buses rattling over broken streets, discordant sirens, impatient horns and the hoofs of the paper collectors' horses. Other sounds began to impinge on her mind. Dogs barked and people blew whistles and called out the wares and services they were offering. Buzzing mopeds pulling trailers of ice cream and baked goods, black taxis with yellow roofs, huge luxury cars and those held together with tape and no glass in the windows raced each other along the impossibly wide highway. There were tiny *kioscos* selling newspapers, gum, maps and *loto* tickets. Walls of public buildings and shops were covered in a potent mix of political grafitti and every spare surface had tatters of old posters and propaganda leaflets, historical wallpaper telling the times.

The streets were swept clean and rubbish was collected each night by a network of ancient ponies and carts. It was taken away to be picked over and scavenged, everything reusable or saleable was rescued. Really recycled. Modern glass-sided sky scrapers lined either side of the avenue bearing the names of international companies and famous hotel chains. Among these were the mellow colours and curly iron balconies of elegant apartment blocks from the last century and fine old colonial buildings. As she walked slowly and drank it all in, Rachel looked up at the skyline and marvelled at the colour and variety and the way that the buildings were crushed together. The streets were lined with trees. The eucalyptus had new silver and ginger bark. The jacarandas were covered in a haze of purple blossom. Lime coloured parakeets shrieked from the centre of the spiky palms. Under the trees were signs that many people lived here, on the street.

There was a background scent of warm, sweetly stewing drains and this was overlaid with the powerfully aromatic smell of meat roasting over large wood fired *parillas*, the argentine barbecue. Rachel stopped to stare at the mounds of beef, pork and *achuras* (offal) sizzling in every restaurant window; whole patagonian lambs were spit roasted, standing to attention around a pit of flame. She remembered that she was extremely hungry and that she must eat before the performance tonight. The hot sun chased her into the dark and fragrant interior.

She loved Buenos Aires. It was her first visit and she was delighted that the company would spend several weeks here so that she could get a feel for the place. It was a big outfit to move around the world: dozens of dancers, stage crew, costumes, props, lighting and, of course, their own ice. The dates at Luna Park had been sold out weeks in advance, their name and reputation ensuring good crowds and rehearsals had been going well.

However, it was an exhausting life. It was fantastic to tour the world and visit new places. They were extremely well paid and well looked after and their glittery costumes and confections of feathers and sequins transported them to other realms and storybook adventures every night. Most of all she loved the reactions from the children when they came to the rink side for a closer inspection. It was certainly exciting and glamorous but physically they worked very hard. Sometimes they had four shows a day and they often skated with injuries. Last month she had skated several shows with a broken wrist. Everyone was permanently tired, jet lagged and displaced. Rachel wondered what else she could do that would ensure such a hit of variety and fun without the frazzled edges.

A squeal from the dressing up box claimed her attention again and she left behind her memories. The children had finished their puppet show so she went to help them climb into high heels and sparkly tiaras. They wove feather boas around their necks and pulled on extravagant, long gloves. This used to be my working wardrobe, Rachel laughed to herself and wondered how the other staff would react if they saw some of her photographs from her previous life. Some of those costumes had been extremely revealing, she conceded, definitely more suitable for international ice dancers than teaching assistants. Martha caught her eye as she turned over the sumptious fabrics in the dressing up box. 'Where did you go this time?' she asked, 'Far East or Latin America?' Rachel grinned and helped Felix disentangle himself from the cowboy suit, 'help me fold them up please Felix' she instructed. They worked together fetching the scattered costumes from around the garden and packing them away into the dressing up box.

'Tidy up time', Martha called from the pergola and everyone helped to clear up and put things back in the labelled boxes. They carefully carried everything down the steps of the garden and deposited them outside the store. Martha lead the ragged line of sun-tired children back into school in time for assembly and going home time. Rachel packed the matching boxes away onto the neat shelves that she had planned and ordered and arranged last year. Everything had its place. She moved a large plastic world globe to the end of the rack and thought about Martha's question. She certainly had plenty of colourful memories to draw on and she would not have missed out on those years for anything, even if it did mean that there were huge chunks of her previous life that she did not share with her colleagues. But did she want to go back? She knew the answer instinctively. This life suited her much better now, she had managed to find something that offered her the fun and variety and even, sometimes, the sheer nail biting terror and adrenaline, of her performing days. It was a nice life. Although of course, it would be quite nice not to have to work at all ...

Is there such a thing as a typical TA? Many tread strange and interesting pathways before they become TAs.

13

Wicked, I love this game!

We are on the landing! It is a nice, airy, bright landing. But it is the landing nevertheless. There are four computers and a printer spread out on the broad shelf under the windows. The sunlight streams in and reflects off the dancing dust caught in its beams. The walls are orange and the doors into adjoining classrooms are a rich eggy yellow. The dark grey carpet looks and smells new. The stairs, on the other hand, are very well worn, dented and scuffed over many years by hundreds of running feet. Opposite the windows, and set back from the stairwell, is a large L-shaped stand which is full of good books, colour coded and inviting.

An old fashioned school bell rings from somewhere far away and there is the jostling sound of lots of children moving around. The school is well kept and tidy, as institutions are when they have enough room for everything and everyone – everyone that is, except the teaching assistant. Her books and folders occupy a corner of the floor where nobody sits, tucked away under the printer. With each sound of the bell she has to move her tables and chairs to make room for the traffic that must flow through her spot on the landing. As children come to join her they move the furniture around in a well rehearsed routine.

Hapi and *Imsety* peer, unblinking, from a wall of Egyptian ceremonial art. Their iconic symbols and motifs are used extravagantly across the pages. The other wall space is used up with rows of pegs and stacks of coats, few of which seem to make it onto the hooks. There is a place for book bags and another for lunch boxes and back packs. PE kit hangs from most of the labelled pegs. The odd school sweatshirt lies crumpled and forgotten in the corner; a mother, somewhere, will be searching her laundry pile in vain, refusing to believe that yet another one has been lost.

The noise from the approaching children increases as they press up the stairs, urgent and giggling. Intent on their friendships and fallouts, they are immersed in this world. It is their society and they are learning to move in it. Here, they are busy with purpose. Some collect instruments and peel off for music lessons, bumping back down the stairs with their guitars or clarinets. Others arrive on errands from neighbouring classes bringing messages and news; lost property and hot property; tickets or rotas for charity events. As the noise quietens again we can hear the noise of water gushing and gurgling through distant pipes and the quiet, mechanical hum from the fluorescent lights. The meaty smell of lunch wafts up the stairs. It smells good.

Jen stands between the classroom and the landing and watches the children settle down. Some are quietly reading or getting on with work, some are choosing new books, and others have brought their playground banter and squabbles into the classroom. Eventually everyone has found their place and registration begins. Jen calls for readers and follows their progress with her own text. There is just time for a few minutes of reading now and these children need a good deal of support and opportunities to read and practise. All too soon they will be leaving this safe junior environment and moving up to high school. Their reading is still poor.

As the class changes over, Jen calls Ralph, her dyslexic student, and they pull out the furniture on the landing. He is working very carefully with paper shapes and paste to make a geometric picture. He is a bright, sunny boy; eager and responsive. Twice a week he attends a dyslexic unit in town for specialist teaching. A link book goes with him between the two schools and there is a folder of worksheets and lists of words to be learned. The special school is driving his learning and Jen supports him patiently, gently. She notices things about the way that he is receiving work and thinking about words and numbers. She knows what he can do and how to help him.

They move on to some extension work with shapes; counting sides and matching names. Repeat, repeat and then move on; small chunks of work and then on to the next activity. She questions and repeats, constantly checking his grasp and understanding, 'is this a regular pentagon – think about it?' Repeat, repeat and then move on. Her session with Ralph is carefully planned, reflecting work done at home, outside school hours. One to one teaching is intensive and exhausting. The pace of the lesson has to be just right, especially with such a short attention span. In a class, or even a small group, different interactions can be planned, between pairs, groups or the whole class. If something does not work, there is always someone else to bounce ideas off; creativity grows organically. The variety of possible activities is far greater and this punctuates and structures the session and aids concentration and assimilation; and when the students are working together the teacher has brief moments for reflection. But between student and teacher there are no such gaps and spaces; the pace is relentless. It is a skilled and costly undertaking. Repeat, repeat and then move on.

The bell rings again and three other boys join Jen and Ralph. They settle down to a worksheet, 'let's get on, if we can get this part finished then we have a game to play'. At last, some interaction! Repeat, repeat and then move on. Jen and the boys carefully study their text. It is painstaking work, pointing out clues that the children do not naturally pick up, prompting, repeating. So gentle.

'Wicked, I love this game!' Ralph's enthusiasm is irrepressible and the four of them throw themselves wholeheartedly into a version of Blockbusters with phonemes in the squares. Their assertions and guesses are wildly inaccurate, demonstrating competitive zeal and scant attention to the patiently repeated rules. After noise and excitement has peaked and interest wanes, she takes them back to the quiet, focused study of speech sounds and word beginnings; she produces worksheets and flashcards and highlighted texts. Repeat, repeat and then move on.

'Can we play that game again?'

'Maybe next time'

'Yessssss!'

We are in our own little world out here on the landing. Sometimes I feel a bit cut off but I do not really mind. I would much prefer to be getting on with my own stuff rather than standing around waiting for someone to notice me. And the materials from the dyslexia unit are easy to use. I really like the boys, Ralph is wonderful to work with and so eager to learn and to please me. I feel as if I am doing something useful and making a difference, more than I would if I were just sharpening pencils or washing pots. While I am here, I do not want to feel in the way. I like to be in control of what I am doing, and to do it well.

The bells ring and the doors of all the classrooms burst open. There is the sound of many doors banging and many chairs and tables scraping across the floors. The peaceful landing is suddenly alive with activity and noise. A wave of children threatens to unseat Jen and the boys as they scramble to move their chairs. They clatter down the well trodden stairs, drawn towards the scent from the kitchen, the sunlight on the playground and the real business of the day.

> Carefully prepared, gently delivered, painstaking one-to-one tuition is another face of TA work.

14

Who would be a teaching assistant?

The research project that informed the stories in this book was carried out over the course of three years that have marked profound and startling change in school workforces. Because of the uncertainty and discomfort that change causes, TAs have been the centre of discussion and argument; information and disinformation; rumour and myth and stories. TAs and their jobs are in the news and under scrutiny. Accordingly, I have included a selection of these notes, clippings, cuttings and headlines in order to capture a flavour of that discourse and to reflect the way that the debate has been worded. It adds texture and further context to the stories.

Teaching Unions leader apologises for 'pig-ignorant' remark
'I said you could not have pig-ignorant peasants supervising classes, but you needed people of good education with appropriate training'
(Garner, 2001)

Warning over 'Mums' Army' in schools
Teachers are warning ministers not to use a 'mums' army' of classroom helpers to overcome the staff shortage and the problem of excessive workload in England's schools. (Eason, 2002)

'I know what I can do, and I know what needs to be done, but I don't always feel I know what is needed' (Juliana, Fieldnotes, September 2006)

'a disastrous scenario' (Eason, 2002)

In terms of what TAs do, while there are issues of taking lessons and registration periods, administering exams and various administrative duties, the most important aspect is still classroom support. In practice, this means:

Persuading students to pay attention to their teacher and stay in the room.

Differentiation, which means explaining what the teacher has said to students who find comprehension difficult.

Motivating the students who, for whatever reason, just can't be bothered.

Supporting students who have difficulty recording their work.

Being possibly the only adult the teacher has talked to all day. (Moore, 2008) (an ex-TA commenting on BBC online-encyclopedia project)

So much of TA practice in the past has been based on implicit assumptions; development of good practice was a question of sensitive TAs picking up what was expected of them and teachers assuming that TAs somehow innately knew what to do. (Watkinson, 2003:56)

Teaching assistants (TAs) are essential – they have been referred to as the eyes and ears of the teacher. They work with teachers, helping with classroom organisation, supporting children with their work and assisting with administrative tasks. (BBC Schools, 2008)

'Keep it up TAs ... you are well worth your salt!!!'

(*Times Educational Supplement* Staffroom, 2008)

For those teachers coming into the profession over the next five years, the management of support roles in their classroom will be a challenging but integral part of learning to be a teacher. Experienced teachers, even those involved in managing teams of qualified colleagues at different stages of their career may find the change to models of teaching and learning with greater involvement of HLTAs and support staff, a profound one. (GTC, 2003)

I absolutely love my job, it is worthwhile and has such variety.
(Learning Support Magazine, 2006:9)

TAs are being forced to cover whole classes even if they do not want to, according to the Professional Association of Teachers, It said TAs were being made to fill in when teachers are absent, sometimes for long periods.
(*Learning Support* magazine, 2006:4)

… it's just nice that someone values what have got to say and wants to share things with you or whatever … yeah as opposed to being told what to do all the time
…
Claire, Fieldnotes, 11.10.2006

'It doesn't matter how good you are at your job or how much experience you've got – if someone says I don't need you – it's undermining isn't it?
I think some of them sometimes feel they don't want to ask you to do something because they don't want you to think they are being bossy'.
(Jen, Fieldnotes, November 2006)

Wanted: One caring, flexible, versatile, intelligent, listening, advice-giving, behaviour-managing, moral-boosting, negotiating, consistent, team-playing individual (who can also make a mean cup of tea).

This could be an advertisement for today's teaching assistant. A little exaggerated, I know, but for all that it includes many of the qualitities that teaching assistants are expected to bring to the job. (Dyer, 2001)

Should the teacher be the only adult in a class?
(An on-line forum debate)

'It's difficult enough being responsible for the kids without having to think of ways to allocate duties to teaching assistants as well. If a teacher has to do all that they may as well not bother having a TA. Having another adult spying on you is hardly a recipe for personal and professional autonomy.'

'It is a shame that teachers are so vilified in the press that some would be defensive about, and feel judged by, another adult in a classroom.'

'I don't object to having a TA; I just genuinely don't see the point of having them. Everything in my classroom is done by me. I prepare the resources, ask a kid to distribute them, teach, and tell the kids to pack away. While they work, I go around and offer assistance. TAs at best are impartial observers.'

'TAs do a damn good job. Just remember, most of them used to do other jobs and so bring in lots of skills. I know of an ex-engineer, qualified to higher national certificate level in both physics and maths, another who was a graphic designer, and a third with an art degree'

(Times Educational Supplement, Staffroom, 20 January 2006)

Researchers found that when extra support staff were employed, teaching staff and head teacher stress decreased, there was more free staff time and pupils behaviour levels improved.
(*Learning Support magazine*, February/March 2006:7)

99

The TAs I studied knew the children that they worked with well, their capabilities, whether the children had 'switched off' and how far they could go for instance in managing behaviour. They talked of the children's progress very professionally, particularly in spelling and handwriting and where they had been closely involved in developing targets and renewing Individual Education Plans. (Watkinson, 2003:27)

I think your stance, thinking about feelings of TAs is so important. I have found on the whole they feel good about themselves and their jobs, usually underestimating their potential and current competency. I think this is largely because of their history – they were invisible – the forgotten staff and now they are exploited. (Watkinson, 2007, personal email communication)

'It's not about weakening teachers' says Clarke (Shaw and Dean, 2004:7)

'The Government has a very clear agenda for schools,' he said. 'Get rid of as many teachers as possible.' They would be replaced by classroom assistants delivering lessons taken from the Internet.

'What they want is education for androids delivered by androids'. (Stewart and Ward, 2004:6)

The Equal Opportunities Commission, Scotland recently began to investigate the employment of classroom assistants in the country's primary schools. Its research shows that classroom assistants are a classic example of how jobs are undervalued when they involve skills linked to the domestic and caring roles that have historically been associated with women. (*Learning Support magazine*, April/May 2006:8)

Early structured phonic interventions, delivered by classroom assistants, should be included as a routine part of school-based intervention as a contribution to school-wide literacy success. (Savage and Carless, 2008:379)

15

Autoethnography

Before dark November is this bright day, golden and fragrant. I turn off the main road into a tiny, creeping farm-lane. Fields stretch on either side, the hedgerows glow with leaves yet to fall and there are blue hills in the distance. I turn a bend and there, amid chewing cows, is a small Victorian school with a neat playground. It is perfect, pretty as a picture, but I approach with trepidation.

One thing leads to another. Morning coffee a few months ago brought me here. Between us, Jane and I had deposited six children at three different schools and nearly been on time. We had filled lunch boxes, found PE kit and signed forms, we had remembered a lot of things for a lot of people. We had walked two dogs in the woods, hung out our washing, done our shopping, organised supper and helped a friend. We had attended to our paperwork and our committees and planned classes for Sunday school and Beavers; and now we felt ready for coffee. I looked around Jane's comfortable and lived-in kitchen as I tipped back in the chair and breathed deeply. The brewing coffee smelled perfect and Jane had a knack of stuffing croissants with chocolate that I had never seen anyone else do. As I rescued mugs from the sink and cleared early breakfast from the kitchen table, I noticed a chalky list of 'To Do's' on her wall: DENTIST!!!; haircuts; fireworks?; recycling; find plasterer; pay paper bill; Tudors project – library books; dog – worms; and then, worryingly, 'Get Job'. She caught my eye, 'I think I have to'.

We talked about money and our time. We talked about having babies and tiny children and how their needs change. We talked about our own needs and the way we spent our days. We discussed money and not having any, we mentioned the need to be active, do something, to make a contribution. We talked about old dreams and new hopes, about being students and getting qualified.

We talked about fitting it all in and the luxury of being able to choose. We talked about a new phase of our lives. We talked about going back to work. 'I will if you will', we agreed. One thing leads to another.

Even so, I approach with trepidation, not really believing that I am about to be interviewed. This feels unreal. What am I doing here and what have I got to offer? I am not nervous but I am not prepared either. How will this be? How will I be? Do I want the job? Can I do the job? I was once a competent adult in a workplace very different from this one, but a dozen years have passed since I relinquished the title of 'employee' and the status and assumptions that go with it: a salary; a pension; annual leave; that 'Friday-feeling' and girly lunches.

> It was noticeable that we dressed a bit more carefully if we were going out to lunch, and paid attention to our hair and make-up. We always celebrated birthdays, promotions and postings, a true Office tradition. There was lunch out and cream cakes for everyone in the afternoon. At 12 sharp we made our exit along the cool-coloured walls and official green corridors. The uniform layout and décor of the Office meant that each floor looked exactly the same. The heavily netted windows and fluorescent tubes created artificial but familiar light. We skipped into the central London street below. Expertly, we picked our way between red buses and black taxis, dodging helmeted cyclists in smog masks and motorcycle delivery riders. Tourists day-tripped across our path, but we used a familiar, hurried gait. We did not go far but collapsed through the unimpressive doors of a neighbouring establishment, our latest favourite. We were immediately engulfed in the warm colours of the bar and the garlicky smell of lunch.

I break away from this wistful place to look at the farmland that hugs the school. I was a very long way from wine bars, girly lunches and central London traffic. The intervening years have been bright and brilliant, shattering and uplifting, undermining and affirming. Sometimes there was isolation, often sleep deprivation and always a steep learning curve. The once competent PA, who always knew exactly how to dress, never lost anything and who flitted through the London traffic at lunch time unencumbered by anything but the tiniest of handbags, had to learn a whole new set of skills. Shockingly, I was not always up and dressed by lunchtime, let alone dressed up. My horizons shrank to a pair of enormous green eyes, a fuzz of black hair and the limitless, un-fathomable potential of the new person before me. The days were full of friends and snacks and naps, hugs and kisses, tiny triumphs and huge frustra-tions: the rhythm and order and routine of being the centre of the universe. My working wardrobe had been packed away, and was now long out of date. It was unsuitable for the daily task of feeding weetabix and mashed banana into a moving target; or the later construction jobs I had, building farms, castles, railways and race tracks.

But the days march on, relentlessly. The milestones mount up and infant days pass. My children do not need me to be at home all day, and the other me, the employee me, wonders what to do next. I found myself reflecting favourably on my previous working life, forgetting completely how happy I was to leave the office on my final day. I missed collegiality; having adult company and colleagues, grown up conversations and being valued as part of a team.

I applied, rustily, for this job and I really do approach with trepidation. My last interview was a long time ago and does not seem relevant. My brand new, sparkly degree in education is relevant. Maybe that will paper over the huge hole in my CV and show that I have not only been raising my children in the last ten years. As if that was not enough ... why always the need to justify what was a really positive decision to stay at home? Modern parenthood is full of guilt: we feel guilty if we work and guilty if we do not. It was bliss to stay at home although sharp tongued sisters sometimes caused disquiet. They were not cut out to stay at home they said, and I felt intellectually deficient because I was. They were climbing the nursery walls they said, driven there by the mundane business of being the centre of the universe. It was better all round if they suited themselves and booted themselves and went back to work. I wondered, 'better for whom?' and bit my tongue and hated myself for being so easily satisfied. They did admire me, they said, for being able to put up with it all. So, while they plumped CVs and built career paths, I built train tracks and lost confidence.

And here I am today, starting again, but what do I have to offer? I have lost my place in the employment market, I have missed out on technological developments, I am out of practice. Who would want me and what can I do these days? I clamp down on these turbulent and pointless musings. I am just dipping my toes into the employment waters I tell myself as I take a deep breath and push open the door.

As a toe-dipping exercise it seems to go rather well, nevertheless I am shocked to be offered the job and am immediately beset by new waves of guilt and feelings of disloyalty. I picture my carefully orchestrated family life falling apart because I work a few hours a day outside the home. Unclothed, unfed and sick children flit through the streets in my mind, unloved and uncared for by this negligent working mother. And never mind all that, what will actually happen if my kids get sick? Again that mummy-tension, who am I? Who do I want to be? Is it about choices? I take a firm grip; I am going to be a teaching assistant for a few days a week, not the Prime Minister. I can probably handle it, and so can they.

'We have some disruptive boys here and we need someone to sit with them during whole class time' said the teacher. I understand the notion of being an extra pair of hands in the classroom. I have been in many infant classrooms as a parent helper and student. I have done nothing but talk to children in the last few years. This much I can offer. I am sure I can do this. They are six years old, how difficult can it be? I am confident.

Confidence wanes. It is months since I was in a school and I am not really sure what will be expected of me. I blame myself for not asking enough questions. My first impression, at the interview, was that the classroom teacher, Vi, was rather nervous and not really enjoying having to cope with the 'disruptive boys'. I had wild visions of taking over, of being asked to stay on – never mind the teacher training! How wrong could I have been? How strange that, in my mind, a 'good outcome' would be to be taken on as a teacher. Where does that prejudice come from? I am starting again, I do not know how to. I do not know who I am, I have been out of the workplace for so long. I am torn between self doubt and self belief: I do not know how to do this, but I cannot help feeling that I want to do more.

From time spent in other staff rooms I know that status is an issue. As a Teacher's Aide in an American school, I never visited the staffroom because I was always on playground duty during breaks. I am not a teacher, and probably never will be, but I do not want to be thought of as less than a teacher. I am ashamed to recognise status issues bubbling up. I would like to enjoy the job for what it is – time spent with children in a stimulating and invigorating environment, but I worry about not knowing as much as the teachers about practical teaching and learning and I worry about looking stupid. I suppose I worry about being someone's assistant even though I made my early career as a 'personal assistant'. How bizarre and fickle these thoughts are. Do I feel I am 'too grown up' to assist anymore? And yet I am not qualified to do anything else. So I worry, too, just a little, about my career. And this is all self induced; no one else actually makes me feel like this!

Autumn term – first day at school
The first day arrives and is brilliant but tomorrow there will be children in school. Today is a planning session with Vi. It is helpful to have time to talk

through the plans and to clarify everything. I wonder whether we will have much time for this once term really begins. The last TA in this class gave written feedback of the day. It is kind of nice to feel appreciated and as if my opinion is valuable too. Vi has written scarily detailed plans. I am stunned by how much paperwork there is and very soon get the impression that primary teaching leaves no time for living a life. Mentally I file this away under, 'Do I want to be a teacher/Why do I want to be a teacher?' Tomorrow seems quite straightforward. The text for the week is *We're going on a Bear Hunt*, one of my favourites. I can do this, we are going to have fun!

Mummy's first day at work is greeted with mild amusement by my own children. They enjoy the novelty. I am worried about the logistics. Two travel to school with Dad; conveniently they all go to the same school. But the youngest is still at the village school, and in order to greet my Year 1 class on time, I need to leave my own infant in a nearly empty playground at an early hour. Friends, as always, plug the gaps but I set off, worrying. As I drive towards my new venture my mind is full of the futility of starting a new career, my lack of confidence about what I can do or offer and the acknowledgement that a large part of me has become rather fond of staying at home.

I feel the physical tug of the distance stretched between me and mine. It is almost painful. I realise that if there is a crisis I will be nearly an hour away; with a jolt I realise that if there is a crisis I will have to ask for permission to leave. Many mini-crises have been avoided in the past (lost kit, forgotten money and permission slips, bumped heads and broken wrists, missing trumpets and recorders and violins, homework still at home) because I have been available to manage them. Always and without question. This little household has had the luxury of someone to shop for food during the day when queues are short. There has been someone with time to clear the laundry, cook a meal and clean the house; someone to walk the dog and collect uniform, text books and clarinet reeds from far off suppliers. They are used to coming home to a house that has not been empty all day. The beds have been made and the mail picked up. When they come home from school the lights are on and the curtains are drawn. Snacks are ready and Mummy is not too tired to help with homework and listen to readers.

All of that is a luxury which comes at the expense of other luxuries of course. Nevertheless, as a system it has worked well for us for many years. I am not the only one who will need to make adjustments. I shift gear and turn back to the conversation with Jane, at the turn of the year. We convinced each other that it was time to do something else. We convinced each other that we needed to move on. I convinced myself that a primary school was my obvious destination. I can do this, we are going to have fun.

I cannot do this. I am not having fun! I have no idea how to get the children to listen to me. I struggle to know how to be or who to be. I am shocked by how naughty some of the children are and what hard work it is for Vi to keep order. They are six years old and yet they take on adult authority all the time. It is exhausting. Even so, when gentle Vi asks, 'what do you think, they are not easy are they?' I try to sound cool and calm in reply. Inwardly I am horrified by what hard work it is – for any of us.

My role is to 'sit on' one disruptive soul in times of trouble and turbulence. Otherwise I support small groups in all kinds of activities. For some of the morning my help is mapped onto the teacher's plans. This is helpful because I know who I will be working with and what I should be doing. I listen carefully to the teacher instructions to the class and fit in, carving out an identity. I am an assistant. I assist. I find, by inference and deduction, the things I need to do. This is not always easy. As a student I had my own agenda and a watching brief, but here I do not know what else I should be doing. After the first week I get the impression that just watching is not enough.

I make a huge effort not to just sit and watch. Although it is all fascinating and I have been trained to observe, I quickly unlearn this skill. I feel, from the beginning, that my presence in the classroom could make a big difference to Vi, as an extra pair of hands. But if I have to keep asking for guidance I will be more trouble than I am worth. I sit with or near the disruptive students and try to develop my own ways of working with them and keeping them on task, repeating or rephrasing things that the teacher says during whole class input in order to keep 'my' children engaged. But I do not want them to miss what she says, or be distracted by my commentary. Often we work with personal whiteboards and so I decide that if I always have one on my lap I can demonstrate spellings or sums as they come up, rather than trying to draw things in the air. It also becomes clear that chasing small boys around under the tables as they crawl away is not a good strategy. Far better to try and make myself enticing company so that they want to stay with me.

During the literacy and numeracy hours I work with a table or group of children. Assisting. Enabling. Often these are the slow starters.

'Come on guys what are we doing today – let's get our things out.

Yes, all of you. What do we need?

Right, do you know what you have got to do?

Off we go then.

Are you OK Karen, do you understand? Col, can you explain to me what you are doing? Yep, and then what?

Guy – pencil?'

It is a small table with seven children working around the edge. The children take their workbooks from the pile in the centre of the table and help themselves to sharpened pencils from the pot. There are rulers and rubbers available too. At one end Guy and Col form a familiar axis of disruption, promoting territorial battles over control of the pencil pot. I crouch between them and we talk about the task in front of them. We read the comprehension questions together and discuss the text. They tell me what they want to write.

'Go on put that then. Col, what are you going to say? Yeah, that's a great answer. Write that and I will be back to see how you are doing. Karen and Jo, how much have you got done?

Dave, you want a spelling ... OK get your spelling book then ... right what do you think it starts with? Listen again, how else do we write that sound? Good, find the page then ... what comes next?'

I circulate, check, crouch down. Encourage, chivvy, chastise. Bend down, stand up, monitor, check progress, question. For five short minutes there is peace at our table, we have stopped fighting over the pencil pot, nobody is pinching or poking or fidgeting. I stare out over the sea of mousey heads. Some are bent over their tables, others are reading scripts together. There is a line of children with floppy books queuing up at Vi's chair. Some tip back on their chairs, gazing into space, hands waving.

'Yes Leo? Bathroom, OK, quickly then. Pete, you can go when he gets back. No, sorry, you will have to wait.'

I look at the clock, ten more minutes, halfway through.

'OK, how are we doing? Karen, you need to get on a bit faster. Would it help if you moved away from Jo? Well, you need to stop talking if you want to stay there. Come on, I need at least two more sentences. Col, where are you at? Guy? No, he's not copying you ... look you have not written the same things! Well, do you want to move? Right, stop fussing and let's read the next question together. Do you remember this bit in the book?'

We settle into a routine. The children are accepting and soon regard me as a regular fixture in their classroom. They do not seem to mind whether their query is answered by me or the teacher, just as long as someone comes. I make a supreme effort to remember their names, it is key to getting their attention. I listen and watch Vi. I absorb her language and techniques. I notice the strategies she uses for answering questions, for encouraging acceptable behaviour and for giving help. I spend a lot of time on my knees getting down beside tiny tables and chairs and people and I climb, bent and wizened, into my car at the end of the day. This is a physically demanding job; I soon learn which outfits are comfortable for life on the carpet. I am horrified by the idea of catching head lice and find girls with long, flicky hair alarming. Mine is short and firmly fastened behind my ears just in case.

It takes time to get my role sorted out and to know where and how I fit in. I feel I should be offering to help people rather than sit in the staff room at breaks. I make a point of trying to get tea and coffee made for people, and of filling and emptying the dishwasher, but usually I am not free any sooner than the real teachers. I am sure they are not expecting me to do it. I am being over sensitive but I find it difficult to know how to be. People are far too nice to ask, but are mine the menial tasks? The telephone in the staff room is an issue: should I be answering it, do they expect me to, could I be any use if I did? I decide to be more proactive. Playground duty is another pinch point, no one likes doing it. Last time I worked as a teaching assistant, about half my time was spent in the playground, but because of my hours, I do not have any to do here. I offered to do one per week on behalf of Vi but she did not jump at the offer, and it is cold out there so I have not pressed her to accept. I do not really feel entitled to a lunch hour.

One break, after a couple of months at school, I staggered into the staffroom, ready for a mug of tea and ten minutes of adult chat. I joined the other teachers, who had been pleasant and helpful, although disinterested in me and mine. The talk in the staffroom was nearly always about naughty children or paperwork, or the impending retirement of three much loved members of the team. Parties were being planned and outfits trimmed. As I reached for the biscuits and tuned into the conversation I began to feel uncomfortable and out of place. The teachers (women who looked like me, sounded like me, dressed like me) were discussing how much they should pay their cleaning ladies. The hourly pay they mentioned was twice the rate I was paid for working alongside them. In a heartbeat I did not feel like one of them any more. I did not feel like a colleague – hard cash evidence said I could not possibly be. I had been ashamed that I thought status might be an issue, but sometimes it just slaps you in the face.

I am piecing together snippets of information about 'my' disruptive child. He is small for his age, with unkempt dark hair. His eyes, dark in a pale face, are lively and laughing but the smallest slight or frustration makes them narrow in anger, foreshadowing cruelty. He is often tired and has a very short concentration span, and he is stubborn. But on our first meeting I am bowled over. He is charming and kind and responsive. We get on well together. He is helpful. Vi and the headteacher are very concerned for him and I am included in the discussion of his tailor-made Individual Education Plan. We plan the strategies that we will use to meet his specific needs and write them on the plan. I will work with him one-to-one on some very basic targets; simple spellings and number bonds and some behavioural goals too. I realise that I do not know how to go about this.

I have no idea what resources are available and there is no time to ask anyone. We muddle through, drawing heavily on common sense. I use the Internet for ideas and we play some games. He is a whiz at 'pairs' and beats me over and over. The plan is that he joins in with whole class work wherever possible. Once he gets wriggly I remove him from harm and we work together. Usually he comes willingly and often asks whether we can work together. I cannot help wondering whether he is being short-changed by my lack of experience and expertise. Is there esoteric knowledge that I lack?

However, within a few weeks he is proud to be able to read the first group of words that we targeted and he demonstrates his newly acquired skill to the teacher and headteacher. We move on, another dozen words and some more complex number bonds. But this flint eyed boy cannot stay an infant; he has to grow up and he is so far from reading and writing that the task seems insurmountable, as it does for him. On bad days he cruises the classroom, under a cloud of frustration. He knows he cannot do what everyone else can do; somehow, somewhere he got left behind. And so he hits out in anger and frustration. But no malice – not yet.

An infant classroom is a place of magic and this one is delightful. If I were to conjure up such a place in my imagination it would look like this. Modern teaching ideas and resources are deployed in a traditional Victorian schoolroom. The ceiling is high, as are the pointy windows. There is space for the sunshine to dance. The walls are cream painted brick, clad in huge bright display boards. There are posters about maths and history and science, maps and diagrams, pies and pie charts. There are school rules and codes of conduct, jolly catchphrases and folklore: the society of the child. The furniture is child size and easily managed – Maria Montessori would be pleased. Resources for every lesson are kept in trays and boxes around the room. There is a comfy library corner provided with squashy cushions and peopled with imaginary friends. Opposite, the vet's surgery is open for business.

I am frustrated by the untidiness of it all. I know that this is a personality thing, and that I find piles of stuff horrifying, but I want to have a good clear-out. The children are not encouraged to keep the room tidy, or rather, they do not do it competently. Some children lose their coats, lunches and PE kit on a daily basis. I dread this! It means I have to approach the huge sprawl of belongings at one end of the classroom. Somewhere under here are pegs with names on but I have yet to see them. Vi's chair is halfway down the room on one side, but there is no desk or place to put a bag. Planning and assessment folders seem to spread outwards from this chair in a haphazard fashion. She arrives and departs each day with at least one huge and heavy box of files and folders in her arms. Originally I thought, 'I would want a desk if this were my classroom' and so I made some attempts to organise small areas but I worried that I might move something vital and upset someone. I do not know the history or the issues. What happened to the last person who tidied up? Instead I ask Vi whether there is any area that she wants me to help with; and then I stop noticing the mess, the system works and there is no time to make a better system.

Because of my super convenient, tailor-made hours (9.30-14.30) I never, ever see a parent. I am a hidden member of staff and it heightens my outsider feelings. I think back to the TAs in my children's classes: they were the most accessible members of the team, highly visible and readily available. I wonder whether the parents know that I work with their children every day and do they care, are they curious?

I stumble through the door at 9.30 each morning, after my own scramble to be all things to all people. The 45 minute drive puts distance between domestic me and employee me. Class, of course, is already in session, Vi does circle time with them, or whole class input, or they do classroom adminis-tration tasks and news. I never get to hear those bits, and sometimes I never catch up. I fold my coat and stow it on the floor in a corner with my bag and keys, find the planning folders and join the circle. I look for my particular charges, I sit near, I join in. 'Mrs Dillow's here', chant Kylie and Karen every morning, and they nestle in against my legs. 'I like your boots/skirt/hair' one of them always confides. They always have a treasure in their laps, something pink or glittery, stickers or purses or hair grips; something so precious that it distracts them from the business of learning and listening. Other girls comb each other's hair, or spend their time moving away from the boys. I am always amazed by how much small children can move when they are sitting quietly on the carpet. You almost do not see it happening, but a mapping exercise would show how they are constantly shape shifting.

Longed-for half term comes and goes and I surprise myself by how much clock watching I am doing. Eventually I have to admit that I am bored. Even though the days are busy and noisy and full, I find the actual minutes of each session seem to creep along. I long for break and then lunch time. I am alarmed to discover this about myself – it is not a nice thing to admit and I try not to. I find this work with young children extremely frustrating. I hate that they do not do as they are told. When they cannot grasp a basic concept I get cross, cross with myself because I do not know how to explain it, and then miserable because I cannot bear another ten minutes bending over their desks. What a horrible person I am. Teachers are angels and so are TAs, and of course the children are too. Just when I think I am about to explode, someone will do something so sweet or funny that you would not want to be anywhere else. I assume that the thrill and challenge of attending to the teaching and learning, planning the lessons and fitting everything in counteracts the tedium for the class teacher; but for the assistant who carries out someone else's plans it is boring. Or is that just me? Now who is climbing the walls?

My role is expanding a little. Despite my reservations about lack of training and expertise there now seems to be an opportunity for me to take small groups away and work with them on my own. This brings its own challenges of control and discipline but it breaks up the day for me and for the children and, presumably, changes the feel of the class that Vi is left with. One thing that I am taking over is 'Guided Reading' which involves small group inter-action with a text. I would really like to see this activity run by an expert so I know what best practice looks like, but there is no appropriate time or money for training. There are materials printed for each batch and level of books but I do need to do a certain amount of planning and preparation for it. I make my own plans, picking out interesting features from the text.

My earlier training to Teach English to Speakers of Other Languages (TESOL) means that they get more than their fair share of phonemes, syllables, tone and stress, and that at least my grammar is sound. For some groups I make worksheets based on the texts and desperately try to think of new and excit-ing ways of approaching the books. I soon learned that bored and unengaged children are innately badly behaved. The stories become terribly familiar, as we begin to run out of books to dissect and discuss, but it does mean that I can recycle preparation notes. I choose and record what I do with each group and how they have coped, and after each group I feed back to Vi. This takes the form of assessing whether the children are in appropriate groups. They seem to get moved around in a very fluid way as we try to get them working at the right level, and so of course very soon half the children have already studied a book in another group. I find even this simple and routine administrative task extremely tiresome and difficult to get right.

Guiding Reading: two tales

Guided reading is a carefully structured approach to teaching reading with a small group of children at approximately the same reading level. Guided reading is a part of a wide reading curriculum.

Guided reading is part of a rich and comprehensive reading programme.

Guided reading sessions aim to encourage children to become enthusiastic, autonomous and thoughtful readers.

www.standards.dfes.gov.uk/primary/publications/literacy

Theory	Practice
Lesson Plan Date **Title**: The Hare and the Tortoise Purple band Group 6 **Materials**: Commonwealth Games props, teacher's text, book set **Targets**: To develop fluent and expressive reading; To encourage careful attention to text in order to increase comprehension; Blended phonemes: air/er/or	'Group 6, are you ready to go with Mrs Dillow? What do they need to take with them today Mrs Dillow?' 'OK, group 6, just a pencil and line up quietly by the door please.' 'Group 6 – can you follow me sensibly please. First of all we need to find a spare room. No Chris, the computer room is full. Rob and Dave, WALKING please. Let's try out here.' We cross the playground and enter the door to the office block.

Theory	Practice
	We walk through the receptionist's office in order to reach the other side of the building. The group is fizzing today, I am not looking forward to this.
	'Quietly up the stairs please, Chris – wait at the top. Gosh it is cold up here.'
	Up on the top floor of the old building there is a warren of small rooms, mostly used for storage. The largest has a table and seven assorted chairs. One is broken. It is a corner office with windows staring out across the carpark to the muddy farmland beyond and the chewing cows. The hedges are frothy with the first signs of spring.
	10 mins
Way in: Talk about races, Sports Day, show Commonwealth Games programme, experiences of running races?	'Let's get going shall we? No, Dave, of course you cannot sit on the broken chair. Rob, over here next to me please. Siobahn can you go there, that's it, perfect. Chris, did you bring a pencil, well why have you broken it?
5 mins	Well you will just have to use half then. Kate do not be silly, get up off the floor. No one else sit on the broken chair. I am putting it outside. Right guys, all you need is your books and your eyes and ears. Pencils down.'

Theory	Practice
	We waste so much time waiting for them to settle down. Why don't they do as they are told – is it me?
	'Who knows what this symbol is? Yep, the Commonwealth Games. And they are happening quite near here – is anyone going? Have you watched any races on the tv? Yeah Dave, they were exciting. Did you see the Marathon? Who has run a race? What did it feel like?
	You did what Chris? No, I do not think you are allowed to do that. There are rules ...
	Is it important to win?
	Our book today is about a race.'
	10 mins
Intro: Look at cover – read title together; Examine picture, predict story type and content, fiction or non fiction? Characters – goodies/baddies. Prompt for 'traditional tale'.	'Let's look at the cover. Can we read the title together ... The Hare and the Tortoise. What are they doing? Who do you think would win if they had a race? No, Chris, the Tortoise cannot ride a motorbike, and he cannot get a piggyback either. It would be cool if he could though! Boys, look at the pictures – tell me what kind of book this is, is it fiction or non fiction? Yes, that's right. What do you think the book is about? You have already read it Katie? in your other group, and you have too Dave? Who else has read it? OK,
Elicit prior knowledge.	
Target questions for comprehension – 'Who was a good sportsman?' (NB cross ref sportsmanship and Commonwealth Games project)	
5-7 mins	

Theory	Practice
	you are going to be brilliant at it then!'
	Oh no, most of them read it last week. How am I going to keep their interest?
	'No, it's not going to be boring. So who can tell me what kind of story this is ... And who do you think is going to win, the tortoise – do not be ridiculous! How can a tortoise beat a hare?
	When we start reading I want you to think about the following question, Who was a good sportsman? Do you remember we talked about being a good sportsman yesterday? What does it mean? Yep, not cheating, yes Siobahn good point, enjoying the game.
	10 mins
Strategies: Go round group – brainstorm ideas for when we do not recognise a word – who will use what?	'Before we start, what strategies are we going to use if we find a word we can't read? Yeah, that's a good one! What will you do Mikey?
Discuss – prediction, sound out, read on, reread, beginnings and ends, chunks	Yep, that will help too, Katie? Rob? They are all brilliant ways of working out a tricky word – good going guys. Any more? Chris, everyone else is working hard here. No, it's not boring if you join
5 mins	

Theory	Practice
	in. No, you can't sit on the floor. You haven't got the broken chair, I moved it. What will you try Chris if you can't read a word?' 5 mins
Independent reading: Silent reading at own pace; Reading out loud to me. (NB notice who is using which strategies) 10-15 mins	'OK, everyone open at the beginning and get going. Siobahn, can you read to me please...' 'Chris and Katie, stop wiggling and settle down, you don't need your pencil at the moment. Leave it alone please. Come on guys – reading – no you haven't finished it already. Chris you can read to me next, where did you get to ...' I don't believe they have finished it already. 'Katie, stop talking – are you stuck?, read forward then and try again ... there you go, excellent.' 'Dave, can you read to me please ...' 'Rob and Mikey, move to this side' 10 mins
Back to text: Praise and feedback to each child – comment on strategies. Discuss – action/plot. Who predicted correctly? Phoneme work – open at page 12/13 – listen to sounds, pick	'Most of you read very nicely then well done! I saw some excellent strategies for attacking new words. Katie can you tell us what you tried – and that worked well didn't it? So, who won the race? Can you all turn to pages 12/13.

Theory	Practice
examples from text: air/or/er NB hair/hare/her Reading out loud together – model fluency, rhythm, intonation and expression. Filler – Read dialogue in pairs. <div align="right">10 mins</div>	We are going to try listening to some sounds and then I want you to pick them out in the text. OK? Here is the first one, listen to what I say and then put your finger on the sound ... Good, and can you see another one? How about this one? Chris and Katie, I am not going to talk when you are talking, listen please.' <div align="right">10 mins</div>
Response: Back to our comprehension question – who was the good sportsman? Why do you think that? (support answer from text). Favourite part? Why? What will you remember about this book? <div align="right">5 mins</div>	'We are out of time guys, Chris and Katie, come back, you must wait for me to go with you. We need to tiptoe past Mrs H's office, she has a meeting in there. Let's go then – WALKING. Did you enjoy the story? What was your favourite bit?' We clatter back to the classroom, the children explode in through the door like a whirlwind. I am exhausted by the effort of keeping them on task for the lesson. I am not sure how well it went. I missed so much out. Now we need to reorganise the groups again. Chris was clearly bored, and so was Katie. It is impossible to find a book they haven't all seen before ... I wonder how Vi copes when she does these sessions.

'I thought, I would really like to see someone doing this brilliantly, just so I know what it should look like.'

'When you see the training videos though, that always gets me when you see the teaching assistant with half a dozen children it is not a real situation half the time is it? Well, my sessions never looked like that! You never get a child that moves out of place or says a rude word and they are always sitting so nicely and they always say the right thing! It's not real.'

(Juliana, extract from fieldnotes, November 2006)

I do not always have the same groups to work with. Sometimes I have those that need extra help with reading or maths and on other occasions I work with those who are moving on more quickly. I realise that this is good planning by Vi; all groups get the benefit of working with the proper teacher in fair measure. Over the course of the week I take groups for reading, ICT and television watching. As we get to know each other better Vi begins to rely on me to run more unusual and creative activities. I try really hard to be self-reliant so that having me around does not create more work for her, but I do have to ask some questions some times.

All the children love to work on the computers and so the group that gets to come and do IT with me is considered 'lucky'! I am not so sure – once again I am pole-axed by my perceived lack of experience. But I can use a computer competently, and my keyboard skills were honed by years of secretarial work, so I do have something to offer.

I show the children how to change the font and colour of their work and to cut and paste text in order to produce a good looking document. I take a group of about ten children into the staff room, which doubles up as the IT suite, and work on various programmes with them. There are also some old, familiar programmes loaded so that if someone finishes early they can play a game. We charge across the corridor, 'walking quietly please everybody!' into the staff room, and I am always relieved if we can have the room to ourselves. This lesson is exhausting. It is noisy because they are working collaboratively, and because they are excited. And they all need help all of the time. I imagine trying to run this with the whole class.

Lovely Vi always seems to be able to do it with a smile on her face and a real appreciation of what the children have achieved. She is great to work with, quietly in control, immensely experienced and knowledgeable and absolutely dedicated to the children in the classroom. She is enormous fun and quietly funny about lots of things. In the normal way, we gradually share bits and pieces of our lives outside school. We have many common experiences because we are both wives and mothers and educated, working women. We are of a similar age. I had wondered what it would be like working as the junior partner.

Teachers who were trained a couple of decades ago were accustomed to having their classrooms to themselves; they were not trained to manage staff. Some find it difficult to direct the work of another adult, particularly another who is the same age as them. In blogs and newspaper forums some teachers object to having other people in the classroom. They say they it is like having a spy in the room, or else it is something (or someone) else to worry about, plan for, organise. I do not want to get in Vi's way, I want to be helpful. She carries off the relationship with great grace and gentleness.

As I learn from her, I respect her as a professional and as a friend. She opens up a little about the burden of the paperwork and administration and I notice that sometimes she seems overwhelmed when yet another new directive comes from the education department. We barely have time to assimilate the latest method for assessment or IT teaching before it is all changed and there are more new forms full of wretched tick-boxes. There is a real feeling in the staff room that the teachers are undermined by this didactic approach to controlling their art. It does not seem to be a particularly positive way of treating professional staff. Mentally, I file this snippet in the ever growing, 'Do I want to be a teacher, or why do I want to be a teacher?'

Christmas

I have always thought that primary schools are very special places at Christmas. We are deeply into our rehearsals and preparation for The Grumpy Shepherd. Our chosen shepherd is indeed very grumpy and does a grand job of stamping her feet and hunching her shoulders. Our innkeeper is rather large and his pants show through his costume. I set to work on the scenery making. I am not really sure how it has been done in the past but I am sure that someone will tell me if I get it wrong. I spend two mornings making cotton wool sheep and stapling them to a midnight blue backdrop spangled with silver stars. The final project looks good and I am proud that it will go up to the local church at the end of term. The children spent some time working on the sheep with me, so some of them look quite monstrous and deformed and quite a few have an odd number of legs. But I made most of them myself. Alarmingly, by the end of the first day sheep and stars are beginning to look rather curly – I think we were over-zealous with the glue. I coach kings and shepherds and soloists in their words and songs. I am not sure what difference I can make, I sing with them and they stare as if I am mad but we make a better sound.

I spend a long time sorting costumes and making new headdresses for the angels and stars. The dress rehearsal goes very well although we all hope that performance nerves will help to quell some of the distinctly unangelic behaviour. I feel guilty that I will miss the performance itself. I do not usually work that afternoon, and my own child has his end of term performance on the very same day, in another school, 25 miles away. I feel I am letting everyone down.

Apparently it was a triumph.

There is a positive buzz in the air today. The children and staff are dressed in their best twinkly and sparkly clothes. I decided not to opt for glitter and novelty earrings, but I did put on my black velvet trousers. We are ready for our end of term Infant Party. I spend the morning wrapping presents and packing snack bags while Vi tries to keep them on task in the classroom.

During the afternoon we organise games and singing. The teachers dance with the children, but I feel a bit awkward. There is a strange, rather dreary atmosphere, an uncomfortable mix of school and party. We are playing games but still stamping on bad behaviour by the usual 'suspects'. I take my lead from the teachers, again working out by inference and deduction how to behave. The children are having a super time and it is lovely to see their faces when our special visitor turns out to be you-know-who! Everyone has a snack bag with soft drink, crisps, fruit and sweets and we retire in small groups for sustenance and to unwrap the gifts that Santa handed out. It is a nice informal time for chatting to the children; just do not ask me to dance with them!

January

After Christmas come the steely months. Everyone gets sick, including teachers and TAs. We pass the coughs and colds, sore throats and upset stomachs around and around. Our own children get sick too and we are torn apart. We want our invalids to stay at home, squished up warmly on the sofa with a duvet and a pile of comics, but we need to send them to school. We go to work and care for other people's children, and other people care for ours. Sweet Vi understands this. Her own children are older and can stay on the sofa unsupervised if necessary but she remembers the tension. Our roles and selves are intermingled and tightly wound, 'Mummy?', 'Miss?'. I look into the fever-bright eyes and pink heavy cheeks of a six year old who should be at home, and my sons' faces dance before me.

Easter Term

Sweet Shrove Tuesday was a good day. When I arrived Vi asked whether I knew how to make pancakes. Fortunately I do. I spent the morning measuring flour and milk, beating batter and tossing pancakes with group after group. Frying butter and citrus oil fill the air. School smells nutty and sweet and sharp, everyone who passes our busy cooking corner asks for a taste. The children are excited by the novelty of the day and the prospect of eating during lessons. In this rural corner of North West England some had never tasted a pancake before and some called them 'crepes' reflecting their more well-travelled experiences. So I teach them how to eat them as well as make them: we sprinkle knobbly sugar from a tatty bag and squeeze fresh lemons, just a few drips. And then we write a recount of the activity, I remind them that washing up was supposed to be part of the deal!

The end of the Easter term approaches and we plan an activity afternoon. I volunteer to make Easter gardens with small groups. We organise a 'circuit' of crafts and activities for them to work on. I raid a friend's stony garden for smooth pebbles to make tombs and begin to collect polystyrene meat trays and tiny bottles and jars. Before the day I take the family into the woods to gather bags of moss and twigs for our landscaping. I have done this many times before. As each group approaches the table we talk about what we are going to do and how; we talk about why and how and remember our Bible story. The children mould hills, bind up rough crosses and collect tiny flowers from the car park to decorate their trays. They spend a blissful time baking and painting and gardening their way around the activities.

At Christmas I had spent a day sorting, folding and labelling costumes from the play, before storing them neatly in the hope that next year they will be easy to identify and use. But I am afraid that I also hoped that next year it would not be my problem. I have been involved in primary classrooms for many years and in various capacities, sometimes paid and sometimes not. They are attractive, compelling and infectious places. They draw me in time and again. I want to be part of the family and part of the fun. The idea of a TA post had been attractive too, it sounded perfect. It offered all the benefits of being involved in the classroom without the huge, bureaucratic load of teaching, or the need to graduate.

Summer term

But in the end, it did not fit, or I did not. The nature of the job was transient, a temporary contract to the end of the school year. As bunnies and bonnets and chocolate eggs replaced kings and shepherds and angels, I gave a half-term's notice. Leaving the children was harder than I imagined it would be. Leaving my special boy was even harder. But he did not hit anyone. He was leaving too, for the adventure of the next key stage. If I had stayed I might have gone with him, but I doubt it. The headteacher, like all headteachers, was grabbing and saving bits of money wherever she could, shuffling around resources and budgets and trying to do her best for everyone. It does not matter how many shapes you make your pot into, you still only have the same amount of clay to make it. So schools recognise that they want and need assistants. And if they have the money in the pot they hire them. But the contracts are often temporary and that affects how assistants feel about their jobs and about themselves. I was sad to leave, but I did not really feel I was letting anyone down. My job may have been advertised again for the new school year. I did not look; I did not want to be tempted.

> This is the rhythm of life in school; day by day, week by week, term by term.

PART 3
DISCUSSIONS

Believing, with Max Weber, that man is an animal suspended in webs of significance he himself has spun, I take culture to be those webs, and the analysis of it to be therefore not an experimental science in search of law but an interpretive one in search of meaning.

(Geertz, 1973:5)

16

Reflection on the data

The stories in this book are about eight TAs and their lives and families and subjectivities. They were written in a variety of styles and voices to reflect the range of personalities and to create a rich and textured text. They use splinters of conversations, quotations and the stories and voices of others so as to build up layers of meanings and understanding. The stories can stand alone or be read in a group, alongside or against each other.

The aim of the project was to show how we, specifically and locally, experienced being TAs and to find an appropriate way of telling about that experience that was organic, subjective and full of dialogue. I do not want to suggest that these are the only ways to experience being a TA, but I can say that this is how it was for us. My reason for writing the research findings as stories was to make them readable and entertaining, but also to share the experiences by inviting you into our lives and settings and contexts. It is a way of creating knowledge. I do not want to tell you what to think about the schools or characters, or what insights or knowledge to draw from them. However, I hope they might have an active, practical purpose. They offer what Ayers has called 'examples of possible lives' – they help us to think, 'here is what someone else has done; what might I do?' (Ayers, 1998:243).

The stories tell of TAs and teachers working together. They show how it feels to be valued, prepared, left to get on with it, daunted, in the way or appreciated. For example, while Claire wistfully reflects on how different her job would be with a little more forward planning and Lois is depressed by the stress of not knowing what is coming up next; Juliana's story shows how effective a TA can be, and how affirmed she can feel, when she is forewarned and forearmed.

Life histories, previous lives and life phases feature strongly as we get to know the TAs and their work. We see them at home and at work, reacting and interacting, coping with challenges and triumphs. Where appropriate I have drawn attention to particular incidents, observations or comments that illustrate good practice or show how better support or working conditions would help. These are emphasised explicitly during this final section. They add colour and detail to current advice for good practice (eg DfES, 2000, 2003). They add another layer to the scrapbook.

The stories we shared had a common thread of 'femaleness'. That is to say: they are stories about women and about the way that women deal with their lives. They are about women's life courses and the decisions that have to be made. They are about women who are workers, students and carers; housekeepers and mothers; cooks or not-cooks; gardeners, sports women, singers and dancers; friends, wives and lovers; grandmothers and daughters. Each of us is a different combination of these labels; or none of them. These women's lives are complex and connected, they carry out demanding roles at work, home, school and community. Their lives are intertwined with their jobs. The stories about going to school, about getting themselves and everybody else ready for school, about leaving their homes like bombsites with a list of domestic chores undone, were similar for all of us (see *Just one more record* and *A class act*).

TAs are always something or someone else too. Being a parent brings another set of complications to the workplace. The following extract from Diane Duncan's book about mature women training as teachers chimed loudly with our feelings about going back to work and study, and the business of fitting it all in.

> Cultural expectations of motherhood and the persistence of gender differences in our society continue to assign the main responsibility for childcare to women. As a consequence, when a conflict of interest occurs between a woman's work and the needs of her children, guilt is often the outcome. One of the difficulties in the women's attempt to keep 'all the plates in the air' was that their lives were so tightly structured that there was no slack in the system to absorb additional burdens. Any 'extra' demands on their time were likely to bring the plates crashing down. Conflict was often at its sharpest when a child was ill and there were taught sessions at college which they felt they should not miss. If they went to college they would feel guilty for sending their children to school feeling unwell: if they stayed at home to look after them, they would feel guilty about neglecting their studies. (Duncan, 1999:67)

The TA (as examined in Chapter 1) is typically female, a carer and often working in her local school where her children are pupils. Claire, for example, is linked to the school and village on lots of levels and she juggles her finite time, carving out space to do everything, often doing two things at once. Blatchford emphasises that the TA profile reflects 'the typical child bearing and rearing phases of their lives' (Blatchford *et al*, 2004:15). The TAs in these stories, and many of those in the bigger, quantitative studies mentioned in Chapter 1, were parents. Their roles, responsibilities and relationships were fixed by the presence of children in their lives. Therefore these stories braid work and life together. The pattern of responsibilities in each life phase feeds into our working lives; it colours our perception and experience and performance. Telling stories helps to capture and record those shifting shapes and colours.

There are, of course, male TAs – although less than five per cent – and TAs who are not parents. Their different lives and experiences will impact on the TAs that they become in just the same way that ours do. Although their stories do not appear here, the general advice and discussion of good practice that follows can be broadly and flexibly applied in a wide range of specific and local situations.

The story form helps to keep meaning making open and personal, but there are some rich general themes which run through the tales and I have drawn these together. These themes reflect advice which was distilled and clearly set out in both the *Working with teaching assistants: a good practice guide* (DfEE, 2000) and advice from the GTC about *Development for teachers working with support staff* (GTC, 2003). Given that the data for this project was collected some five years after the publication of those documents it does not seem unreasonable or superfluous to draw attention to the advice once more.

Advice for TAs

These stories have been written to show the lived experience of teaching assistants. From them it is possible to answer the question, what is it like to be one? Prospective TAs could read the stories and imagine themselves there, in the classroom, dealing with the situations. This might help them decide whether it is a path they wish to tread – it provides material to think with. It might also be that TAs already in post find ideas here for ways they could improve their position, standing or circumstances.

■ What type of person makes a good TA?

A good TA needs a wide set of skills and qualities. Obviously she needs confident numeracy and literacy skills and a genuine passion for working with young people. She will also need endless patience and charm and kindness. She will need to be fit and flexible. She will need to think on her feet, make things up as she goes along and be willing to do the same thing day after day. She needs to be able to act, paint, dance and sing. She has to be good with guinea pigs and computers; she should be very, very tolerant. In a well run school and department she should feel secure as part of a professional team, valued and appreciated. She should feel interested and challenged by each day; confident enough to tackle new tasks and practise old ones. She may need to survive boredom or sheer nail-biting terror. Every day will be different because people are different and children are different.

■ What is it like to be a TA?

The stories show that the work of a TA is varied and interesting. It is physically demanding, mentally stimulating and emotionally satisfying. However, situations vary enormously depending on local conditions and personal relationships. It could be the most exciting and perfect job, but that depends on the school and on the way staff teams operate. Most TAs love their jobs – they display a very high level of job satisfaction. The TAs in this study all agreed that the job suited them perfectly. They liked the close association with their local communities and valued the school holidays and working hours which fitted in well with their other commitments. They would have liked to earn more money but although TAs do not think they are well paid, the amount is more or less what they expect to be able to earn.

> 'The money – it would be nice if it were a little more but the school only has so much money so if they paid you more per hour you would only be offered fewer hours.' (Ellie, Fieldnotes, June 2006)

They also love their lives outside school and appreciate that they have the time and energy to enjoy them.

Some TAs move very quickly on to promotion or to teacher training. Many stay happily for years and by doing this they contribute, immeasurably, to the teaching and learning of those around them.

> She believes passionately that schools need TAs who are good at being assistants and who do not want to train as teachers. But they do need to be recognised as professional people in their own right and not just as would-be teachers. She believes that the best thing for the child is to have a teacher, teaching, and an assistant, supporting. (Reflection on conversation with Deborah, Fieldnotes, April, 2006)

■ Drawbacks?

There are of course situations and relationships that are not positive, fulfilling and productive. Negative issues usually stem from locally experienced tensions. Not all partnerships work well. Some teachers are nervous or threatened by having another adult present in their classroom. Sometimes the need for a TA has not been planned for or communicated carefully and so boundaries and job descriptions are blurry. This can lead to a stressful working environment, for both teacher and TA. Induction and training can ease these stresses. However, more entrenched views will be tougher to resolve. Not everyone welcomes or values TAs; not everyone knows what they are for or how to use them.

In some schools, support staff, including TAs, have been added ad hoc when extra funds have become available. In these cases job descriptions might be muddly or ill defined. They may have grown organically as different TAs have taken on different bits and pieces of responsibility. TAs may work all over the school, flitting from class to class when needed. The TAs in this study found these roles difficult to negotiate. Their job satisfaction definitely increased when they felt secure and were involved in ongoing contact with a class or year group.

■ Also consider

Two other factors which affect the nature of the role are the age range of the children and the size of the school. The feel of the job changes completely with the age of the child. Foundation and Key Stage 1 assistants will spend lots of time helping with the practical and physical skills that children new to school need to learn. A TA in these years will need to be patient with helping children to dress and undress, manage in bathrooms and at lunch time. She will need to be good at shoe laces, Velcro and plaits, and very good at finding lost property.

The size of the school also makes a difference to the scope and feel of the role. Small schools and small staff teams usually mean that all staff, including TAs, take on a wider variety of tasks so there is more opportunity to offer particular skills. There may also be the opportunity to carve out an interesting niche with more responsibility, as Martha and Rachel did at Chantry School. On the other hand, a bigger school may well offer more structured career routes and training opportunities. There will probably be a more clearly defined TA team offering the possibility of peer support and interaction.

Summary

Are you interested in being a teacher's assistant who offers general support as required by a teacher or group of teachers? Or would you like to be a teaching assistant who directly supports learning in the classroom?

- When you visit the school, look carefully at the working environment. Notice how the TAs and teachers are working and talking together, are TAs involved in the class or sitting on the sidelines. Do they handle their tasks, material and pupils confidently? Ask about opportunities for training and development.

- Look at the school noticeboard, website and other printed or published material, for example a prospectus or handbook. Are the TAs named and recognised as part of the team? Do they have specific roles or are they general helpers?

- Check that the nature of the job suits you. Do you want to be involved closely with a class or group, or would you relish the variety of moving around the school, stepping in whenever and wherever needed?

- Think carefully about the ages of the children you would like to work with. What do those children do in school?

- Look at the size of the staff team. How many TAs are there and how are they organised?

Advice for schools

The TAs in this study represent a spectrum of family responsibilities and commitments to the wider community. Their lives are full. They are content with the choices they have made and with their work life balance. They indicated, for example, that they would not want to become teachers because, 'we want a life and to go home at the end of the day' (Martha, Fieldnotes, March 2006). They stated that the job suited them because it enabled them to fulfil their other commitments as well those to their employers (Jen, Ellie Fieldnotes, 2006).

However, their dialogue and stories show that because of the delicate balance between their lives and their work, they do need some assurances about their employment. They need to know where they stand, for example, regarding time off in lieu of extra hours worked, payment or support for staff development and paid (or unpaid) attendance at staff meetings.

The relationship between a school and its support staff is important. The stories in Part 2 give colourful examples of relationships that work well and those that do not. The following advice is drawn directly from these experiences and stories. It has been distilled into a series of points to consider and questions to ask.

▧ Recruit carefully

Before everything, there needs to be carefully considered recruitment; have you found the right person for the tasks you are expecting of them? Chapter 1 outlined the diverse nature of TA roles and highlighted the difference between a teaching assistant and a teacher's assistant. It is likely that the two roles will demand very different person specifications.

Secondly, have you got an authentic job for them to do? Job descriptions should be updated and precisely drafted to reflect the scope of the role. Blurry boundaries make people feel edgy and unsure. Grey areas are not helpful.

▧ Eliminate grey areas

Are the practical things like hours, holiday pay, duties, attendance at meetings and inset clearly agreed and clearly communicated? Are contracts agreed and understood? The TAs in this study were on permanent contracts. This helped them to feel committed to developing their roles. However, it was hard for them when they did not know which classes they would be attached to in the new school year and unnecessary resentment was stirred up because it made them feel less valued. Was there any reason for NOT telling them, was it an oversight, or was it assumed that they would know?

> We really, really want to know where we will be next year. The teachers all know what they are doing and where they are going next year. There would be uproar wouldn't there, if they didn't know what classes they were teaching? Or how many hours they were doing, it is the middle of July now!' (Ellie and Claire, Fieldnotes, July 2006)

Magic at the Manor illustrates how quickly good will and a positive experience can turn sour because of a simple, practical matter. It snatched the magic from the day. The TA had taken equal responsibility for the children on the trip. Her duties had mirrored those of her teacher colleague. The storytelling deliberately mingles the teacher and the TA in order to emphasise the parity of their roles and responsibilities on this day. She had worked several hours extra and this was the second, identical trip of the week. She was not there to have fun, she was working. Trips should not be 'a bit of a grey area'; neither should support staff feel awkward or embarrassed about claiming for overtime. These systems should be established and clearly communicated to all members of staff. It is helpful if administrators and secretaries also know who is entitled to what so that they can handle requests from support staff sensitively and appropriately.

■ Provide clear deployment

Mujis and Reynolds (2002) pointed out that standards will not rise just because TAs are there; they need to be trained and deployed properly. TAs need clearly defined roles and responsibilities in order to become effective members of staff. Objectives should be specific and clearly communicated. Does the TA know what she is doing and why? Does she know how to assess or evaluate the task? In other words, how does she know whether she has achieved her objective? Does she know where to go for help and is there space in her timetable to seek help? Has she had time to prepare resources and read through notes, rehearse even? Ofsted's evaluation of school workforce reform highlights the importance of clear deployment,

> The most effective support was provided when teaching assistants received high quality training relevant to the needs of the pupils and were clear about the purpose of their support and intervention. (Ofsted, 2007:21)

Sensitive supervision is important too. Is she comfortable with the amount of responsibility? If she is constantly seeking approval or permission does she lack confidence, training or information? Is she attached to an appropriate line manager, for example a class teacher, year group or key stage co-ordinator or SENCO and does she know who it is?

There are stories here about TAs standing on the sidelines and wondering what to do. Claire felt underused and ill prepared for her classroom experience (see *Just one more record*) and many of the participants in my study reported feeling like this. At Pinetrees, tensions had arisen because some staff did not make full use of their TA time.

> Well I just knock on doors and say hello, can you use me – I usually find something to do! (Fieldnotes, Claire, July 2006).

They had also mentioned that sometimes their presence was unexpected, unplanned for or not wanted.

> It doesn't matter how good you are at your job or how much experience you've got, if someone says, 'I don't need you' it's undermining isn't it? And teachers do not necessarily know what you can do, and it is hard if they are not even expecting to have you in their classroom. (Jen, Fieldnotes, September 2006)

Watkinson has pointed out that, 'so much of TA practice in the past has been based on implicit assumptions, development of good practice was a question of sensitive TAs picking up what was expected of them and teachers assuming that TAs somehow innately knew what to do' (Watkinson, 2003:56). As TAs we often needed to make it up as we went along. We watched teachers and teaching and built up a repertoire of methods that worked. We mirrored their strategies and echoed their voices, finding out by trial and error how to be. This level of flexible thinking and adaptability is a valuable skill, but none of us liked being caught out without preparation.

> I didn't know what activity I was doing until the teacher said ... right the Orange group are going off with Mrs X and then I would think, Oh, right that's my job then! (Claire, Fieldnotes, September 2006)

We all developed and used mechanisms to get through the day, much like the coping strategies that have been identified as part of the art of teaching (Hargreaves, 1978; Pollard, 1982). We used them to fill the gap between the terrifying moment when you learn that you have to do something that you do not know how to do and actually having to go ahead and do it.

'Coping' is a concept that has been used in the traditional analysis of the sociology of teaching. It is a way of examining an individual's relationship and interaction with his or her society, the culture of the classroom. It pinpoints the actual point of interaction between a person and his or her work. These stories help to show what coping means and how it feels, for individuals. See for example Claire's moments of 'blind panic' as she did not know what to do or say, or Martha's reference to 'busking it'.

There are also practical reasons why TAs need information about the day ahead. At Flatlands, I enjoyed our pancake morning but I would not have done if I had never made a pancake before; particularly since there was no opportunity to learn a recipe or practise. In *The wrong shoes* Lois had a miserable day, just because she had not been forewarned about the trip. Appropriate equipment and clothing make it easier to do a good and effective job. This story reflects the accounts that TAs made about arriving in class to find the children putting on their coats ready to make a trip. Why were they overlooked? How did the information pass them by? Forward planning would enable them to play a fuller and more effective part in the day's activities. It would help them to feel part of the team.

■ Create teams and enable partnerships

Working relationships are important because they affect our everyday lives and experience. They affect the type of employees that we are, they affect the way that we think and feel about our work and ourselves, and they affect the way that we approach each day. They also affect how we are able to cope with circumstances.

Being part of a team is vital for effective practice as well as for contented, fulfilled staff.

There are simple, practical steps that help to encourage team building. Are new TAs introduced and inducted? This is important even if the TA is already a parent helper. Colleagues, governors and parents need to be informed about the official change of status. New TAs should be shown the simple things like where to hang their coats and how the coffee machine works. Is there a staff-room coffee club? Are they included? Staff rotas, distribution lists and registers should be amended and TAs should be included on school web pages and in the prospectus so that they are officially recognised and valued.

> I think that parents are shocked when I send a letter home – you know – could you help your child with this please. Well, who is she to tell me what to do?

> I think they feel a bit like that sometimes. (Rachel, Fieldnotes, May 2006)

Teamwork relies on communication. The teacher-TA team is vital and communication between the two is paramount. Is there time for this to happen? TAs are often used to enable teachers to take advantage of planning, preparation and assessment (PPA) time but there also needs to be time for the teacher and TA to have PPA time together. This may be just a few minutes daily and then a longer session regularly for medium term planning, but it does need to happen. Look at the effective partnership between Juliana and the teacher in *A class act*. They check back with each other regularly so that they can assess, review and fine tune. It is part of the rhythm of their day. Ofsted says.

> Where the teacher and the teaching assistant had carefully planned the work together, teaching assistants were often given a high level of responsibility within lessons, and regular activities. (Ofsted, 2007:21)

If the TA is included in the planning stage, or at least has time to discuss the teacher's plans, she will understand what she is doing and why. At Flatlands, Vi included my tasks in her weekly planning, and asked for feedback at the end of the session. These times should be preserved and protected as far as possible; once term starts everyone is overstretched and too busy, and good intentions fall by the wayside. As Rachel and Martha comment in *Tell me what happens*, 'but it never happens, this is an infant school, it's never normal is it? Something comes up'.

Apart from lesson planning, it is also important that teachers and TAs have time together to share information about pupils. Is there time to discuss assessment, reading book levels or individual education plans? The TA is a key member of the team, Her insights from small group work or one to one sessions are invaluable.

It is important, too, for TAs to have time to meet together. This helps them to feel empowered in the workplace and it encourages them to reflect on their practice (Collins and Simco, 2006). When transcribing the data for this study I noted that the TAs spent a lot of time discussing practice between themselves. They were reflecting on teaching and learning. TAs feel empowered when they work in circumstances which offer them ready training and support and when they are offered time for collaboration and professional dialogue. It helps them to construct positive attitudes and meanings in their working lives. According to the non statutory guidance issued under the *Every child matters* framework, the ability to reflect and improve, to share information and to work in teams are seen as core skills that need to be encouraged and developed throughout the children's workforce (DfES, 2005). Is there a time and a place for TAs to meet? Can this time be ring fenced and protected so that they feel encouraged to reflect and critique? The sessions I had with the group of TAs at Pinetrees were valued by them as a time to reflect on their practice and they decided to ask their headteacher for a specified meeting time in the future.

> J: One of my questions last week at college was about feedback and you know, do you get time to plan and discuss your work and, lastly, did we get time for TAs to meet. And there wasn't very much room but I added this paragraph on the bottom saying that we had done this thing with you and that four of us had met and brought up issues and different things.

> E: Because the only time that we meet is in the Staff Room when the staff have gone to get the children from the playground and then we have a quick word.

> C: Otherwise we are whispering and feeling like we shouldn't say anything.

> CD: I really like this idea of TAs meeting together, because you are discussing teaching and learning and it is a way of being professional and sharing ideas etc...

> Yeah (general agreement) – shall we do that then?

> J: Yes, shall we have one each week even after Celia has gone?

> E: Yeah, I wouldn't mind, it'd be good, helpful.

> C: We wouldn't need long would we?

> (Juliana, Ellie, Claire, Fieldnotes, October 2006)

Whole school partnerships are important. These can be encouraged through staff meetings, whole school inset and inclusive communications. If possible invite TAs to staff meetings and inset sessions and pay them or give them time off in lieu if these occur outside their normally contracted hours. Think creatively about ways to include them; do they have special skills or specialist knowledge that they could share in an inset session (eg English as an additional language (EAL), a relevant second language, signing or Makaton, first aid)? Make use of them. They represent a wealth of diverse experience and knowledge, a precious resource that effective managers and schools do well to recognise and utilise. The TAs in this study wanted to keep up to date and to improve their knowledge and skills. They wanted to feel valued as part of the staff body.

TAs will be involved in other partnerships too. They may have easy, natural relationships with the parent body and often play a vital representative role during school functions such as the Christmas Fayre and the Summer Fete. The TAs in these stories worked with other community groups such as the local churches and uniformed organisations. These links help to embed the school into the local community.

There also need to be clear lines of communication between TAs and specialist outside bodies, for example the ethnic minorities service or EAL providers. In *Wicked, I love this game!* Jen communicated directly with the dyslexia unit via a link book that was carried by the student.

◼ Development and training

The 2007 Ofsted report and evaluation of the school workforce emphasises the importance of training to successful staff teams (Ofsted, 2007).

> One of the greatest challenges facing school leaders was to provide an increasingly diverse workforce with relevant induction, training, performance management and professional development to contribute to an identifiable career structure. (Ofsted, 2007:5)

Chapter 15 reports the discussion I had with Jane about the options that suited our new life phase. Implicit in this dialogue is an understanding that, at some level, we wanted or needed to work, 'to do something'. Work is a prime activity in adult life and is associated with healthy personalities (Astin, 1984). The TAs in this study took pleasure in their work and were interested to progress and develop their careers. They wanted to do a good job. They wanted to be useful. They wanted to feel that they were part of the team and kept in the communication loop. They wanted to learn and develop transferable skills and they wanted support in this. *A class act* and *Just one more record* show Juliana and Claire fitting in studying for their courses and demonstrates the value they place on being well informed. Claire directly associated learning from her course with improved job satisfaction,

> I feel I am enjoying it much more now I am doing this course – you relate what you are doing to what you have learnt. (Claire, Fieldnotes, October 2006)

Several of the TAs highlighted the need for transferable qualifications, something concrete to take away should they need to move on. Career development is measured by regular performance review. Have they had the opportunity to discuss their progress and to receive formal recognition of their achievements? Do they need help and support to identify areas of strength and weakness? Do they know when they were doing a good job and what they could do to improve their practices and skill sets?

The TAs in this study enjoyed the opportunities to develop specialist skills such as first aid, ICT or mathematics. They cared about the learning of the children and wanted to improve their own skills so that they could do a better job. The notion of these jobs being merely a bit of extra pocket money for bored housewives is wide of the mark indeed.

Teachers may need training too. Teachers training now will encounter units about management of support staff and working with teaching assistants but they may not have had experience of managing other adults. When considering a teaching career they may not have thought about it. Those who trained before the changes to the children's workforce may feel equally unprepared for the presence of another adult in their classroom. Watkinson says, 'Teachers have not often in the past been trained to work with additional adults in the classroom, and sometimes find that planning work for them, managing them as well as pupils, and taking account of their views merely adds yet another burden to the workload' (Watkinson, 2003:121). It is someone else to perform in front of.

National standards for training teachers require that trainees learn how to deploy, plan for and manage additional adults in the classroom and that newly qualified teachers (NQTs) should reflect on these abilities when thinking about and planning their own development. The GTC recognises the importance of this training for NQTs and also for more experienced teachers. It recommends that early professional development (EPD) and continuing professional development (CPD) should emphasise how important it is to get these relationships right (GTC, 2003).

Hancock noticed in 2001 that teachers themselves wanted more teamwork training (Hancock, 2001), they need opportunities to develop their professional skills in these new directions. It is my hope that by reading stories of TAs and their lives, teachers may avoid feeling threatened and that classroom relationships may start well and flourish soon into supportive and affirming partnerships. This must lead to happy, healthy classrooms; it must impact positively on teaching and learning.

Summary
- Recruit carefully. Keep job descriptions up to date. Ask WHO do you want?
- Avoid grey areas around hours, duties, meetings, holidays and inset. Ask HOW will they fit in?
- Provide clear deployment, well defined responsibilities and sensitive supervision. Ask WHAT will they do (and why)?
- Create strong teams and partnerships. Ask WHEN can they meet together?
- Review performance and enable training and development. Ask WHERE do they go next?

17

Reflections on the research methods

I wanted to show feelings. Is that possible?

Surveys and questionnaires do not show feelings.

A Likert scale allows for some mild gradation of response but it does not capture feelings – pain, joy, frustration, boredom.

How do we understand another person's feelings?

How do I know what your day is like?

How do you know my life?

I tell you, you tell me. We choose the words.

We make our lives public by telling stories.

This is what happened to me today.

Can you feel it?

If you can feel it, perhaps you can understand it.

I believed firmly, right from the outset, that telling stories was an appropriate method to choose for this research project. We live storied lives. The stories we tell are the way we share our experiences. It is the way that we catalogue, remember and attempt to make sense of our personal and collective lives. Sometimes that sharing is carefully crafted and edited, at other times it is instinctive and natural. It was therefore natural to use storying when studying peoples, lives and cultures. It enabled me to write about people in a free and natural way which could honour the wayward, fickle and surprising way in which we manage and share our lives and our relationships. I was able to display, 'concern for understanding how people actually get through the day, the week, and the year' (Delamont and Atkinson, 1995:47).

We told stories about working in classrooms, sharing jokes and anecdotes. How else do you know someone else's life? Their stories and their recollections were so vivid that often I could put their real words into the heads or mouths of their fictionalised counterparts. I crafted their stories, but they had already crafted them. Let us not forget that.

> People shape their daily lives by stories of who they and others are and as they interpret their past in terms of these stories. Story, in the current idiom, is a portal through which a person enters the world and by which their experience of the world is interpreted and made personally meaningful. (Connelly and Clandinin, 2006:477)

We all edit and analyse as we share our lives. We decide the stories we are going to tell. There is no telling it as it is, there is only telling it as we saw it and felt it and understood it, and then we choose how to tell it depending on our context. The choice of storytelling as a methodology reflects this editing process that we all do, with all experiences.

I wrote stories from the material I collected and from my own autobiography. This helped me to move flexibly between them and me. I could include all that I had experienced in primary classrooms in order to build up layers and texture. I could use voices to represent different personalities and standpoints. I tried to make stories that sounded like our conversations, chatty in nature, revealing and vulnerable and honest. When they spoke about standing on the fringes, not quite sure how to proceed, or about worrying about what to say to the children and whether they would behave for them, I could share that vulnerability because I had been there too.

> If anyone else sought to study my life ... no amount of interviewing or observation of me by a researcher would have been capable of producing the depth, richness, and fullness of data I was able to assemble via fully-immersive (and documented) self-observation, self-interviewing, and self-analysis. (Vryan, 2006:407)

Not just anecdotes

This is research data that looks like anecdote, or even fiction. I have called it storytelling, but what is there that makes it reliable? Clifford Geertz, writing about anthropological authors and 'being there', suggests that it is the inclusion of 'fine detail' that makes the writing believable (Geertz, 1988:13) and Bochner calls for concrete detail (Bochner, 2002). Bruner said that a good story convinces of 'lifelikeness' (Bruner,1986).

I have tried to be lifelike. I have offered stories which have details about smells and colours and sounds. I have expressed everyday hopes and fears and feelings. I have talked about dreams. I have documented days in ten minute intervals and included flashbacks to earlier lives. My characters have spoken in their own words and phrases, sometimes unedited and unpolished, reflecting the unfinished and imprecise way that conversations really happen. One conversation became a script. Martha and Rachel, who really had been performers in other lives, were like a double act and I wanted to capture the pace and rhythm of their speech. They were eloquent and funny and dynamic, they finished each others sentences and they knew each others thoughts. When I played back the recording to them and they read the transcript they laughed out loud, delighted. They wanted to show it to their own audiences, they said their husbands were always asking, 'what do you actually do?' We made it into a script and they performed it again, just for fun.

The methods I have used to tell these stories are designed to share and build knowledge by creating feelings and emotions. How then should they be evaluated? Along with Van Maanen, Denzin, Ellis, Bochner and Richardson, whose stories, lives and techniques have inspired and informed my writing and research, I want my readers to decide:

- Do the stories make you want to respond?
- Do they allow you to feel specific situations and unity of experiences?
- Did I penetrate your hearts and heads?
- Do you grapple with the ways you are different from and similar to me?
- Do they show what life feels like now and what it could mean?

18

Conclusion

One thing leads to another. I am sitting in my study reading the stories the TAs have told me and that I have written. I can hear their voices as I read their words. I think of the friendships that started, the bits of our lives we shared, the honesty and the trust. The descriptions of the schools and the children replay vibrantly in my mind. I can see them and feel them and hear them. I read again my own story and relive it. I feel the frustration and the tedium, the joy and the fun. I stand again at the big old sink, with the hot tap running, scrubbing paint from the stained and worn palettes, and see my hands turn red under the running water. I splay the bristles of the fat paintbrushes and watch traces of primary colours swish down the drain. I groan at the dark paint on my pale sweater and under my fingernails. Then I turn and look at the printing we have finished this week. The groups filled in their final layer of colour today and all of a sudden, as if by magic, their designs make sense and what had looked like an artless mess now has shape and meaning. They have turned out well.

One thing leads to another. I remember the cards and notes the children made when I left. There were funny drawings, sweet cards full of glitter and stickers, touching words written with screwed up faces and clenched hands. There were pictures of me with eleven fingers and three hairs. Precious memories. But is that all this is about – nostalgia? Is all of this any more than personal and trivial? Why would anyone else be interested? A reader, a 'critical friend' asked, 'it may be well written, evocative, original, compelling, enlightening: but so what? What have you achieved?'

My initial aim was to investigate the lived experience of TAs, and I found that our daily experiences were inextricably linked with the bigger picture. And so I have shown the background and context against which these stories are played out. Examples of lived experiences can help with reflection or, rather, they provide material to think with. They show others coping or not coping, they show how it could be. They show alternatives and possibilities, 'here is what someone else has done; what might I do?' Sometimes, such insight can be emancipatory. Claire and Lois both moved forward after reflecting on the experiences of others. Claire, Juliana, Jen and Ellie valued the forum we created for sharing ideas. During our sessions they regularly exchanged information and intended to keep meeting together after the end of my data gathering sessions. We learn from the lives and experiences of others. Reading and writing those stories is one way of enabling the information to be shared. At other times lived experience is not so active, but it can help counter feelings of isolation. Someone else is in the same boat. There is value in that.

The stories of lives are useful in another way too. They help to show culture – these lives show the culture of the primary classroom. They give tiny details that can be stuck together in a variety of ways to create an impression of schools and what happens in them. This reflects my view that writing about me, or them, in the culture is a way of writing about the culture. Primary schools are a familiar environment; we have all had something to do with them. Most people have a view about what should be going on in them, or about what is going wrong in them. However, for many people, modern primary schools are not familiar. If they have contact with them it is usually to leave their children or grandchildren at the gate. They are welcomed in as visitors on special occasions, for meetings or concerts or exhibitions or cake sales. Stories of lives and experiences offer a glimpse inside. One thing leads to another. It may be that lived experience and stories from lives give a perspective about educational issues that cannot be obtained through other sorts of research. Primary schools are often in our headlines. We worry about declining standards, test results and poor behaviour. We worry about children learning the basics of mathematics and grammar, and we worry that they are not eating healthily. Stories of lives on the inside give us material to think with.

TAs are often in the headlines too. Teachers and teaching unions worry that they are being used as non-qualified substitute teachers; TA unions are worried that they are being exploited as teachers on the cheap. Reading the stories of TAs' experiences adds another perspective to the attention grabbing headlines, they help to fill out the information available about what TAs are doing and how they are doing it. We could look (for example) at the stories of Juliana or Jen or Deborah in their classrooms and decide whether we think they could stand in for the teacher if necessary. We could compare that with other stories we have heard about the shortcomings (or otherwise) of supply teachers. We might read the stories of overburdened and stressed teachers, and think about having Claire or Martha or Ellie in the classroom. Would they feel like spies or angels? We could read the dialogue between Martha and Rachel and use that to think about the support staff remuneration debate. Stories give us material to think with in subjects that are topical and relevant to many of us.

Stories of lives are important to us culturally too. There has been a huge rise in the popularity of 'fly on the wall' documentaries, and biographies have enduring power. Schools have also provided a rich backdrop for many novelists and scriptwriters, for example Charles Dickens, Alan Bennett, P G Wodehouse, Evelyn Waugh, J K Rowling and Muriel Spark. These two interests, in lives and in schools, combine in the popular fiction genre of stories from schools. Here, educational research collides with the story world. Schools are interesting places and the classroom, its characters and its business provides seams of interesting material and inspiration.

These stories are an attempt to share the experiences of TAs. And TAs are very important. They are important because they are at the heart of a process that is vital for our society. They have been entrusted with an important role in teaching and learning. They are an intrinsic part of the school workforce reform and are tied up with raising standards. Other studies have looked at how effective they are and how they might improve; these stories show how TAs experience this and how they are living with it.

By reading this book you have spent some time in an unfamiliar story world, you have peeked into the storybox. We have shared our lives and our stories in order to paint an evocative picture of the primary classroom and our small part in it. At the end of it all I remain committed to the use of stories to represent lives, and committed to the use of stories from lives to understand cultures. If you now feel you know more about being a TA than you did before you started, then the stories have indeed worked their magic.

> The idea is to draw an audience into an unfamiliar story world and allow it to see, hear, and feel as the fieldworker saw, heard, and felt. (Van Maanen, 1988: 103)

Sequel

This study has concentrated on the stories of lives. And after the data gathering and writing up, those lives go on. So what has happened to my small cast of characters since I left them?

Our Fairy Queen, Martha, continues to juggle her family commitments in the real world of work and routine. She gets up at 5 each morning. These early hours are her time, for meditation and reading and preparing her soul and body for the world. She rouses her tumbling boys (bigger now, of course) from their beds and gently wakes her sleeping daughter. She plaits hair, makes breakfast and lunch and sees them off to school. Then she starts her half hour walk to work. This is the time that she uses to think about the day before her. Her days are different now, the storybox records a fracture in the routine. Her soulmate, Rachel, has moved on and no longer shares the space, the days or the tasks with her. Martha found that she, too, needed a change and so now she is back at school herself. Finally she has the time and energy to formally study the Fine Art that she has been practising for so long – it is the next act in the story of her life.

For Rachel, life has changed beyond belief. A year ago she gave birth to a precious baby girl. Her days are now full of friends and snacks and naps, hugs and kisses, tiny triumphs and huge frustrations: the rhythm and order and routine of being the centre of the universe. She is loving it all, making the most of this unlooked for and unexpected joy. She is proud of baby Rose, who is clearly the most talented and extraordinary child anyone ever met. She is relishing every milestone and putting off, for as long as possible, her return to school. Eventually, of course, her experiences as a mother will bleed into her experiences as a TA. Her baby girl will start school and Rachel will find that she cannot separate out her TA self and her mummy self. She should not.

At Battlefield the young head has moved on and an acting headteacher is in place. The school was inspected in 2007 and, in a good report, special reference was made to the effective deployment and skills of the TAs. Deborah has finished her accreditation as an HLTA and also her Open University degree. She wants to continue in this place, because it fits in with her commitment to the local community, but she has also been exploring other opportunities. She finds that she has a heart for working with the elderly, after all these years with young people. She finds similarities in the skill sets she needs for the two age phases. There is also a learning support position at the local prison that is interesting. In the meantime, she directs the walking bus to school: an orderly snake of local children who meet at her house each morning to be fluorescent-vested and escorted a mile down the hill to school. And there is the small matter of the narrowboat that she and her husband optimistically bought a few years ago. Perhaps they will spend the next few years exploring the sedgey byways and towpaths of middle England's inland waterways instead of working.

Up the road at Pinetrees, Juliana, Claire, Jen and Ellie are all still in place. The new Headteacher has settled in and the rhythm of life at school, in the bubble, has moved on and become routine. Claire has finished her NVQ3 and is so, so proud of herself. It has made a huge difference to her confidence and the way she approaches her work. She understands much more why she is doing what she is doing and that helps everyone.

Juliana is halfway through her Foundation degree. She continues to work effectively with Miss Rose. They are a gorgeous, fabulous and stylish team. She thinks about teaching sometimes, knowing that she could move on to teacher training once she graduates. But she is aware of the huge bureaucratic workload that goes with it and is not sure that she has the stomach for it. One thing leads to another; she will wait and see what happens. Her children are growing up and moving on, both of them have finished with primary school now. She wonders whether she ever will.

For Jen and Ellie nothing much has changed, and for that they are grateful. Their children are grown up, their husbands are nearly retired, they are happy and satisfied where they are. They do a good and sound job in their class-rooms, building up knowledge of the children as they come up through the school. They are part of the fabric of the place, offering precious continuity. They have taken their place in the story box.

References

Ainscow, M (2000) Poor tactics let down mums' army. *Times Educational Supplement,* 31 March 2000, p24

ASC, (2006) *Statistics of education: school workforce in England,* id ref VO2/2006, National Statistics, www.dfes.gov.uk/rsgateway (accessed 19.09.2006)

Astin, H S (1984) The meaning of work in women's lives, *Counselling Psychology,* 12(4) pp116-126

Atkinson, P (2006) Rescuing autoethnography. *Journal of Contemporary Ethnography,* 35(1) pp 400-404

Ayers, W (1998) Biography and the public voice in Kridel, C (ed) *Writing Educational Biography,* London: Garland Publishing Inc (pp 235-244)

BBC (2008) http://news.bbc.co.uk/2/hi/uk_news/education/7462691.stm (accessed 25.06.2008)

BBC Schools (2008) www.bbc.co.uk/schools/parents/life (accessed 27.02.2008)

Bass Jenks, E (2002) Searching for autoethnographic credibility: Reflections from a mom with a notepad in Bochner, A P and Ellis, C (eds) *Ethnographically speaking,* Walnut Creek: AltaMira Press

Birkett, V (2001) *How to survive and succeed as a teaching assistant,* Wisbech: LDA

Blatchford, P, Bassett, P, Brown, P, Martin, C and Russell, A (2004) *The role and effects of teaching assistants in English primary schools: Results from the CSPAR KS2 Project,* DfES Research Report 605, Institute of Education: University of London

Blatchford, P, Bassett, P, Brown, P, Martin, C, Russell, A, Webster, R. and Haywood, N. (2006) *The deployment and impact of support staff in schools: Report on findings from a national questionnaire survey of schools, support staff and teachers,* Brief No RB776 June 2006, Nottingham: DfES Publications

Blatchford, P, Bassett, P, Brown, P, Martin, C, Russell, A, and Webster, R (2007) *Deployment and impact of support staff in schools*: Report on findings from the second national questionnaire survey of schools, support staff and teachers (Strand 1, Wave 2 – 2006), DCSF Research Report RR027, Nottingham: DfES Publications

Bochner, A P (2002) Criteria against ourselves. In Denzin, N K and Lincoln, Y S (eds) *The qualitative inquiry reader,* Thousand Oaks, CA: Sage (pp 257-265)

Bruner, J (1986) *Actual minds, possible worlds,* Mass: Harvard University Press

Burnham, L (2003) *The teaching assistant's handbook,* Oxford: Heinnemann Educational Publishers

CACE (1967) *The Plowden Report: Children and their Primary Schools.* A Report of the Central Advisory Council for Education (England) London: Her Majesty's Stationery Office

Clandinin, D J and Connelly, F M (2000) *Narrative Inquiry: experience and story in qualitative research,* San Fransisco: Jossey-Bass

Clough, P and Nutbrown, C (2002) *A student's guide to methodology: justifying enquiry,* London: Sage Publications

Coffey, A (1999) *The ethnographic self: fieldwork and the representation of identity,* Thousand Oaks: Sage Publications

Collins, J and Simco, N (2006) Teaching assistants reflect: the way forward? *Reflective Practice,* 7(2), pp197-214

Connelly, F M and Clandinin, D J (2006) Narrative inquiry. In J L Green, G Camilli and P Elmore (eds) *Handbook of complementary methods in education research.* Mahwah, NJ: Lawrence Erlbaum.

DCSF (2008), School Workforce in England January 2008 (provisional), Statistical First Release 10/2008, London: DCSF

Delamont, S and Atkinson, P (1995) *Fighting familiarity: essays on education and ethnography,* New Jersey: Hampton Press Inc

DfEE, (2000) *Working with teaching assistants: a good practice guide,* London: Department for Education and Employment

DfES, (1998) *Teachers meeting the challenge of change,* London: Department for Education and Skills

DfES, (2001) *Every child matters: change for children,* London: Department for Education and Skills

DfES, (2002) *Consultation document: developing the role of school support staff,* London: Department for Education and Skills

DfES, (2003) *Raising standards and tackling workload: a national agreement,* London: Department for Education and Skills

DfES (2003b) *Developing the role of school support staff: analysis of responses to the consultation document,* Runcorn: DfES Consultation Unit

DfES (2005) *Common core of skills and knowledge for the children's workforce,* Nottingham: DfES Publications, DfES/1189/2005

Duncan, D (1999) *Becoming a primary school teacher: a study of mature women,* Stoke on Trent: Trentham Books

Dyer, L (2001) The highs and lows of a teaching assistant. In O'Brien and Garner (eds) *Untold stories: LSAs and their work,* Stoke on Trent: Trentham Books, pp83-88

Eason, G (2002) *Warning over 'mums' army' in schools,* http://news.bbc.co.uk/2/hi/uk_news/education/1906038.stm (accessed 04.07.2006)

Ellis, C (2004) *The Ethnographic I: a methodological novel about autoethnography,* Walnut Creek, CA: AltaMira Press

Ellis, C (2007) Telling secrets, revealing lives: relational ethics in research with intimate others. *Qualitative inquiry,* 13(1) pp 3-29

Ellis, C and Bochner, A P (2003) Autoethnography, personal narrative, reflexivity: researcher as subject. In Denzin, N K and Lincoln, Y S (eds) *Collecting and interpreting qualitative materials 2nd Edition,* Thousand Oaks: Sage Publications

Garner, R (2001) Teaching union leader apologises for 'pig ignorant' remark. In *The Independent,* 17 November 2001

Geertz, C (1973) *The interpretation of cultures: selected essays,* London: Fontana Press

Geertz, C (1988) *Works and lives: the anthropologist as author,* Stanford: Stanford University Press

Gerber, S B, Fin, J D, Achilles, C M and Boyd-Saharias, J (2001) Teacher aides and students' academic achievement. In *Educational Evaluation and Policy Analysis,* 23 pp 123-144

REFERENCES

GTC (2003) *Development for teachers working with support staff and HLTAs: Advice to the Secretary of State and others*, GTC, www.gtce.org.uk/shared/contentlibs (accessed 02.07.2006)

Hancock, R, Swann, W, Marr, A and Turner, J (2001) *Classroom assistants in the primary school: employment and deployment*, ESRC funded project: R000237803, The Open University

Hargreaves, A (1978) The significance of classroom coping strategies. In Barton, I and Meighan, R (eds) *Sociological interpretations of schooling and classrooms*, Driffield: Nafferton

HMI (2002) *Teaching assistants in primary schools: an evaluation of the quality and impact of their work*, HMI Report No 434 April 2002

Holman Jones, S (2005) Autoethnography: making the personal political. In Denzin, N K and Lincoln, Y S (eds) *The Sage Handbook of Qualitative Research 3rd Edition*, Thousand Oaks: Sage Publications pp 763-791

Howes, A, Farrell, P, Kaplan, I and Moss, S (2003) The impact of paid adult support on the participation and learning of pupils in mainstream schools. In *Research evidence in education library*, London: EPPI-Centre, Social Science Research Unit, Institute of Education

Hrniewicz, L (2007) *Teaching assistants: the complete handbook*, Norwich: Adamson Publishing

Kearney, C (2005) In search of some answers. In Conteh, J, Gregory, E, Kearney, C and Mor-Sommerfeld, A, *On Writing educational ethnographies: the art of collusion*, Stoke on Trent: Trentham Books (p151-165)

Kessler, I, Heron, P and Bach, S (2005a) 'You're an assistant, assist!' comparing assistants in education and social care, Paper presented to ERU Conference, Cardiff Business School, September 2005

Kessler, I, Heron, P and Bach, S (2005b) *Assistant roles and changing job boundaries in the public services*, End of Project Research Report, ESRC Award: Res-000-23-0069

Lee, B (2002) *Teaching assistants in schools: the current state of play*, LEA Research Report 34, Slough: NFER

Lee, B and Mawson, C (1998) *Survey of classroom assistants*, Slough: NFER

Learning Support Magazine (2006) Letters Summer Term 2006, London: Brightday Publishing (p9)

Moore, B P (2008) www.bbc.co.uk/dna/htg2/A13045024 (downloaded 27.02.2008)

Moyles, J and Suschitzky, W (1997) *Jills of all trades: classroom assistants in KS1 classes*, London: ATL

Mujis, D and Reynolds, D (2003) The effectiveness of the use of learning support assistants in improving the mathematics achievement of low achieving pupils in primary school. In *Educational Research*, 45(3) pp 219-230

Neill, S R St J (2002) *Teaching assistants: a survey analysed for the National Union of Teachers*. London: NUT.

Nixon, J (2005) Good teachers? The integrity of academic practice. In *London Review of Education*, 2(3) pp 245-252

NJC (2003) *School support staff: the way forward*, London: Employers' Organisation, www.lge.gov.uk/conditions/education/content (accessed 09.05.06)

O'Brien, T and Garner, P (2001) *Untold stories: learning support assistants and their work*, Stoke on Trent: Trentham Books

Ofsted, (2005) Inspection Report www.ofsted.gov.uk/reports *, accessed 01.04.2008

Ofsted, (2006) Inspection Report www.ofsted.gov.uk/reports, accessed 15.07.2008

Ofsted, (2007) Reforming and Developing the School Workforce (October 2007 – Reference no 070020), www.ofsted.gov.uk , accessed 15.11.2007

Ofsted, (2007b) Inspection Report www.ofsted.gov.uk/reports *, accessed 15.07.2008

Ofsted, (2007c) Inspection Report www.ofsted.gov.uk/reports *, accessed 15.08.2008

Polkinghorne, D E (2007) Validity issues in narrative research. In *Qualitative Inquiry*, 13(4), pp471-487

Pollard, A (1982) A model of classroom coping strategies. In *British Journal of Sociology of Education*, 3(1), pp 19-38

PWC (2001) *Teacher Workload Study: Final Report 5 December 2001* www.teachernet.gov.uk_doc932ACF19E2.doc (accessed 27.02.2006)

Savage, R and Carless, S (2008) The impact of early reading interventions delivered by classroom assistants on attainment at the end of Year 2. In *British Education Research Journal*, 34(3), pp 363-385

Shaw, M and Dean, C (2004) It's not about weakening teachers, says Clarke, *Times Educational Supplement*, 16 April 2004, p7

Smith, P, Whitby, K and Sharp, C (2004) *The employment and deployment of teaching assistants (LGA Research Report 5/04), Slough: NFER*

Stewart, W and Ward, H (2004) Report on debate at the NUT's Harrogate conference, *Times Educational Supplement*, 16 April 2004, p6

TA Forum (2008), www.ta.forumup.org (accessed 27.02.08)

TAWG (2001) Teaching Assistants Working Group, *Roles and career development of support staff in pathfinder schools*: Discussion Paper, London: DfES

TDA (2007) Training and Development Agency for Schools, *HLTA professional standards*, www.tda.gov.uk/support/HLTA/professstandards (accessed 26.11.07)

TDA Press Releases (2008) *Support staff spur increase in teacher job satisfaction* www.tda.gov.uk/about/mediarelations/2008/280208.aspx (accessed 19.08.08)

TES Staffroom (2008), www.tes.co.uk/section/staffroom (accessed 27.02.08)

Van Maanen, J (1988) *Tales from the field: on writing ethnography*, Chicago: The University of Chicago Press

Vryan, K D (2006) Expanding analytic autoethnography and enhancing its potential, *Journal of Contemporary Ethnography*, 35(1), pp 405-409, http://jce.sagepub.com (accessed 23.04.2007)

Watkinson, A (2003) *Managing teaching assistants*, London: RoutledgeFalmer

Whitty, G (2006) Teacher professionalism in a new era, text of the first General Teaching Council for Northern Ireland Annual Lecture, 14 March 2006, www.ioe.ac.uk/directorate/GTC-NIAddress (accessed 20.11.2007)

Wilson, V, Schlapp, U and Davidson, J (2002) *More than 'an extra pair of hands'? Evaluation of the classroom assistants initiative: final report* (Edinburgh, SCRE).

Wilson, R, Sharp, C, Shuayb, M, Kendall, I, Wade, P and Easton, C, (2007) *Research into the deployment and impact of support staff who have achieved HLTA status*, Slough: NFER

Woolfson, R C and Truswell, E (2005) Do classroom assistants work? In *Educational Research*, 47(1), pp 63-75

* Unique reference numbers removed to preserve confidentiality

Index